Ten-Minute Plays for
Middle School
Performers

Plays for a variety of cast sizes

Rebecca Young

MERIWETHER PUBLISHING LTD.
Colorado Springs, Colorado

Meriwether Publishing Ltd., Publisher
PO Box 7710
Colorado Springs, CO 80933-7710

www.meriwether.com

Editor: Theodore O. Zapel
Assistant editor: Audrey Scheck
Cover design: Jan Melvin

Library of Congress Cataloging-in-Publication Data

Young, Rebecca, 1965-
  10-minute plays for middle school performers : plays for a variety of
  cast sizes / by Rebecca Young.
       p. cm.
  ISBN: 978-1-56608-158-0
  1. Middle school students--Drama. 2. Teenagers--Drama. 3. Young adult
drama, American. 4. One-act plays, American. I. Title. II. Title: Ten-minute
plays for middle school performers.
    PS3625.O969A615 2008
    812'.6--dc22
                      2008028803

  1   2   3   08   09   10

Dedication

This book is dedicated to my daughter, Ashley Gritton, who helped write two of the plays: "What's Her Name?" and "Overbearing Mother" (which she swears is *not* about me!). I couldn't have done it without her! Proving that having a middle school daughter is 99 percent inspiration and only 1 percent frustration! (OMG, JK — you know I heart you, 4-ever!)

Table of Contents

Introduction

Many middle school performers are uncomfortable taking the stage by themselves. Who can blame them? Acting solo can be very intimidating! That's why ten-minute plays are perfect for younger actors. Ranging from duos to groups of up to seven or more, these plays offer short but age-appropriate material and themes.

All the themes used in this book reflect the interests and issues of teens today. Some will make you laugh; others will make you cry ... and just a few have a little of both! You will find a wide variety of material to choose from. Don't worry about inappropriate language either. This book was written with teachers and students in mind! Nothing to cause that all-too-familiar middle school giggling. Well, at least not too much! (Who knows for sure how a middle school mind works?)

These plays all stand alone. Each one is approximately ten minutes long. Girl and guy parts can be changed if necessary, and in some cases more parts can be added. With a little creativity, you can make any of the plays work for you!

Props can be used but aren't necessary. Often it's more interesting (and fun!) pretending (or even improvising) than actually using a prop or piece of scenery.

So what are you waiting for? Grab a friend — or two — and take the stage! You'll be so glad you did!

How to Be Popular in 10 Days

(4 Girls)

CHARACTERS:

    Tasha: Girl who buys a "How to Be Popular in 10 Days" kit.

    Erin: Skeptical of the kit at first, then gets excited.

    Millie: Friend who is skeptical and also a little "blonde."

    CD Voice: Female who will be the voice of the CD. She looks straight out at audience, not at the girls On-stage.

SETTING:

    Erin's bedroom. She and Millie are sitting around when Tasha comes rushing in. When the CD is played, the three girls do not look at the CD voice; they act as if the voice is coming from the CD player.

1 *(TASHA enters carrying a box.)*
2 TASHA: It's here, guys! It finally came! *(Rushes over to girls On-*
3   *stage.)*
4 ERIN: What? What finally came?
5 MILLIE: *(Sarcastically)* Let me guess, another tacky sweater from
6   your grandmother?
7 ERIN: Ooooh. Remember that yellow one she got last year? It
8   was *hid-e-ous!*
9 MILLIE: That was nothing compared to the one she got the year
10   before ... wasn't it orange and pink?
11 TASHA: Guys! Forget about the sweaters! This, my friends, is
12   not a sweater!
13 ERIN: Then what is it?
14 TASHA: It's my very own "How to Be Popular in 10 Days" kit!
15 MILLIE: Your what?
16 ERIN: Are you kidding me?
17 MILLIE: Come on! Please tell us that you are kidding! You did
18   *not* just say, "How to Be Popular in 10 Days"? *(ERIN and*
19   *MILLIE laugh.)*
20 TASHA: Fine. If you're not interested, I'll just go open it at my
21   house. *(Starts to walk away, knowing that they're going to*
22   *change their minds.)*
23 ERIN and MILLIE: *(Pause for half a second then yell.)* **Wait!**
24 MILLIE: *(Rushes over to TASHA and pulls her back.)* You know we
25   were only kidding! Of course we want to see what's in your
26   "How to Be Popular in 10 Days" kit.
27 TASHA: That's what I thought. *(She tears into the package and*
28   *starts pulling out items.)* Look! A CD!
29 ERIN: *(ERIN grabs CD from TASHA and starts reading from the back.)*
30   "Tired of being invisible? Getting shoved into the lockers
31   as people push past you in the hallway? Then this kit is for
32   you! Is it fair that all the hot guys are snatched up by the
33   popular girls? Of course not!"
34 MILLIE: Amen, sister! *(Grabs CD and finishes reading the back.)*
35   "Take charge of your destiny! Stop envying those popular

1   girls! By following the steps on this CD, you can beat those
2   girls at their own game. In just 10 short days, your school
3   will be saying, 'Who is *that* girl?'"
4 ERIN: Wait! Isn't that what they're saying now?
5 TASHA: Very funny. Stick that baby in the CD player and let's
6   see what we've got! *(ERIN takes the CD from MILLIE and puts*
7   *it in the boom box. They settle in to listen.)*
8 CD VOICE: *(Booming voice)* **Hello and** — *(Very quickly, ERIN hits*
9   *stop because it is so loud.)*
10 ERIN: Whoa! That's a little too loud, isn't it? Where's the volume
11   on this thing? *(She fiddles with the buttons and then hits play*
12   *again.)*
13 CD VOICE: *(Normal sound level)* **Hello and welcome to the first**
14   **day of your new popular life!**
15 ERIN, TASHA, and MILLIE: Hello!
16 CD VOICE: Ready to get started?
17 ERIN, TASHA, and MILLIE: Yes!
18 CD VOICE: Everyone knows that the first step to being popular
19   is to be friendly. In fact, one might say that friendliness is
20   the best friend of popularity.
21 ERIN: *(Hits pause again.)* Is she kidding me? "Friendliness is the
22   best friend of popularity"? What kind of horse manure is
23   she shoveling?
24 TASHA: Just give it a chance. I'm sure it's going to get better.
25 MILLIE: Yeah. Hit play and let's see what she's got.
26 CD VOICE: So let's practice being friendly. Give me your biggest
27   smile. *(ERIN, TASHA, and MILLIE smile widely.)*
28 CD VOICE: Great! Now tilt your head to the side to give yourself
29   that perky little cheerleader look that all the boys love.
30   *(ERIN, TASHA, and MILLIE tilt and smile.)* **Awesome. Now, to**
31   **be popular you'll want to get the boys' attention. So while**
32   **you're still smiling and tilting, give your hair a little flip over**
33   **your shoulder.** *(ERIN, TASHA, and MILLIE smile, tilt, and flip.)*
34   **That's right! You're working it! Now smile, tilt to the other**
35   **side, and flip your hair with your other hand.** *(ERIN, TASHA,*

1   *and MILLIE smile, tilt, and flip on the other side.)* **Perfect. Now**
2   **let's practice that all together.** *(Girls try to keep up as the*
3   *voice on the CD tells them what to do.)* **Smile. Tilt. Flip.**
4   **Smile. Tilt to the other side. Flip. Do it again. Smile. Tilt.**
5   **Flip. Smile. Tilt to the other side. Flip. Make sure you're**
6   **smiling your biggest, friendliest smile.** *(ERIN hits pause on*
7   *the CD player.)*
8 ERIN: Ow! I think I pulled something in my neck.
9 TASHA: I'm feeling a little dizzy.
10 MILLIE: I could do this all day. *(She keeps doing it while talking.)*
11 TASHA: *(Rolling eyes and still rubbing neck)* **Blondes.**
12 ERIN: Gotta love her.
13 MILLIE: Come on, guys. Hit the play button! *(ERIN hits play.)*
14 CD VOICE: Let's move on to step two. An important part of
15   being popular is to speak the jargon.
16 ERIN: *(Very skeptical)* **The jargon?**
17 CD VOICE: Repeat after me. "Girl, you look phat in those
18   jeans!"
19 TASHA: Girl, you look phat in those jeans!
20 MILLIE: Wait! Hit pause. *(ERIN hits the pause button.)* **I don't think**
21   calling people fat is going to make us very popular.
22 ERIN: Seriously, Millie. You are so blonde sometimes. She
23   means phat. P-H-A-T.
24 MILLIE: Oh, yeah. I knew that. *(Clears throat.)* **Girl, those jeans**
25   make your thighs look so phat! P-H-A-T! *(ERIN and TASHA*
26   *shake their heads. ERIN hits play again.)*
27 CD VOICE: Let's try another one. "O-M-G, you are totally my B-
28   F-F!"
29 ERIN, TASHA, and MILLIE: O-M-G! You are totally my B-F-F!
30   *(Whenever ERIN does what the CD says, she's more or less*
31   *making fun of it. She is definitely not buying into the whole*
32   *thing.)*
33 CD VOICE: Great! Let's try another! "Dang! I haven't seen you
34   in a minute, girl, where you been?"
35 ERIN, TASHA, and MILLIE: Dang! I haven't seen you in a

1   minute, girl, where you been?

2 ERIN: *(Hits pause again.)* Is she kidding me? Nobody I know talks

3   this way!

4 MILLIE: Duh. That's because we're not popular! Turn it back on.

5   I think I'm starting to get it. *(ERIN rolls eyes and hits play*

6   *again.)*

7 CD VOICE: OK. Let's try this last one. Repeat after me: "Did

8   you see — insert name of boy here — at the game? He is

9   all that and then some!"

10 ERIN and TASHA: Did you see Jack at the game? He is all that

11   and then some!

12 MILLIE: *(She says it at the same time as ERIN and TASHA only she*

13   *doesn't actually insert a boy's name but repeats it exactly as is.)*

14   Did you see — insert name of boy here — at the game? He

15   is all that and then some! *(ERIN hits pause as she and TASHA*

16   *break into laughter.)*

17 MILLIE: What? What's so funny?

18 ERIN: *(Obviously sarcastic)* O-M-G, you, my B-F-F, are totally

19   stupid!

20 TASHA: Yeah, does the B in B-F-F mean "blonde" for you,

21   Millie?

22 MILLIE: What did I do?

23 ERIN: *(Mimics her.)* Did you see — insert name of boy here — at

24   the game?

25 MILLIE: Well, that's what she said.

26 TASHA: You were *actually* supposed to say a boy's name.

27 MILLIE: Oh. Well, maybe she should've made that clear.

28 ERIN: I think she did. *(Laughs and hugs her.)* Don't worry. We

29   love you anyway!

30 TASHA: Yeah. You're all that and a bag of chips, Millie! *(Hugs*

31   *her, too.)*

32 ERIN: Oh, she's pure butter, dawg.

33 TASHA: She's my homey-g, for shizzle!

34 MILLIE: All right. Knock it off! Just hit the play button and see

35   what else she's got. *(ERIN hits play as they settle back in.)*

1 CD VOICE: OK, now that we've got the friendly look and the
2 talk, it's time to walk the walk. Everybody on your feet.
3 *(They all stand.)* Now to be popular, you've got to know how
4 to walk. Heads up. I mean, really up! Those other students
5 are beneath you. They're pond scum. You won't waste your
6 time looking at them. You've got bigger fish to fry. *(The*
7 *three girls put their heads up as she speaks.)* Now get those
8 shoulders back. You want people to take notice of you,
9 don't you? Don't be slumped over like a bum on the side of
10 the street. *(The three girls put their shoulders way back.)* Now
11 get moving. Strut it out. Give that booty a little shake.
12 That's right! Get those hips moving! Do you want people
13 noticing you or not? Shake that booty! Shake that booty!
14 You are the most popular girl in school! You want people to
15 notice you! Keep that head back! Shake it! Shake it!
16 Shake it! *(As the voice is calling out, the three girls prance*
17 *across the room. All three should really exaggerate their*
18 *movements. TASHA and MILLE because they are really trying,*
19 *ERIN because she's making fun of it all. Then they collapse to*
20 *the floor pointing and laughing at each other.)* Keep moving!
21 You can do it! You *can* be popular! *(ERIN, still laughing,*
22 *crawls over to CD player and hits pause.)*
23 ERIN: Omigosh! You should've seen yourself, Tasha! I don't
24 think I've seen that much hip action since the year they
25 made us hula in gym class! It was hilarious!
26 TASHA: Me? What about Millie? Her nose was so stuck up in
27 the air; I'm surprised she doesn't have a nosebleed!
28 MILLIE: I thought I looked pretty good. You have to project
29 confidence, you know!
30 ERIN: I don't think that was confidence you were projecting.
31 MILLIE: What about you? You looked like a drunken soldier
32 walking around on wobbly legs!
33 ERIN: I know! That's what I was shooting for!
34 TASHA: So you say. But I've seen the way you *really* walk, and
35 believe me, this isn't that far off!

1 ERIN: Very funny. I think you're just mad because you wasted
2   money on this stupid kit.
3 MILLIE: It's not stupid. She makes some very valid points.
4 TASHA: Besides, we haven't even finished it. Maybe she saved
5   the best for last. *(She walks over and hits play.)*
6 CD VOICE: All right. We've got the friendly smile, the tilt, the
7   language, and the walk. Now it's time to look the part! Go
8   to your kit and take out the catalog enclosed. *(TASHA*
9   *rummages around in box and pulls out a catalog. The other two*
10   *girls look over her shoulder as she flips through it. While the*
11   *VOICE on the CD talks, the GIRLS point things out to one*
12   *another in obvious shock and disbelief.)* **To be popular, you**
13   **need to be aware of the latest trends in fashion! You should**
14   **never walk out that door wearing less than the best! The**
15   **only way to get people to stop and take notice is to actually**
16   **give them a reason to stop. So grab a pen and start circling**
17   **your favorites! This is your *life* you're talking about. Now is**
18   **not the time to be cheap! You didn't think popularity came**
19   **without a price, did you? Of course not! Nothing in life is**
20   **free! Make sure you accessorize from top to bottom. Don't**
21   **forget, we take all major credit cards. So what are you**
22   **waiting for? Fill out those order forms and begin your life of**
23   **popularity today!**
24 ERIN: Does that say fifty-nine ninety-nine for a tank top?
25 TASHA: Look at these pants — they cost more than a prom
26   dress!
27 MILLIE: Oh man, I can't afford clothes like this!
28 TASHA: Who can? If this is what it takes to be popular, I think
29   I'm going to have to go back to being invisible.
30 ERIN: You're not invisible to us.
31 MILLIE: Yeah, who needs this stupid kit? *(Pushes box to floor.)* **So**
32   **what if we're not going to be popular in ten short days!**
33   **We'll be unpopular together!** *(The three hug and walk off.)*

The Legend of Bloody Mary

(3 Girls)

CHARACTERS:

Carrie: Teenage girl who gets scared easily when baby-sitting.

Bridget: Teenage girl who loves scary stories and doesn't scare as easily. She tries to scare the other two with her Bloody Mary story.

Hannah: Teenage girl who also gets scared easily.

SETTING:

The three girls are at Bridget's house for a sleepover. They are sitting around telling scary stories and decide to try the age-old Bloody Mary story.

1 CARRIE: What about the one where the claw ends up on the
2   trunk of the car?
3 HANNAH: That one freaks me out!
4 BRIDGET: My favorite is the one where the security guard at the
5   mall dresses like an old woman and then tricks you into
6   helping him —
7 CARRIE: And then he hacks the girl up with the handsaw and
8   stuffs her in the trunk! Gory!
9 HANNAH: The absolute worst one is the one where the killer is
10   already in the house and he keeps calling the babysitter.
11 CARRIE: Yeah. That one *really* creeps me out.
12 HANNAH: *(Looking around nervously, says to BRIDGET.)* You did
13   lock the door, didn't you?
14 BRIDGET: Don't worry. This is a safe neighborhood. Nothing
15   ever happens around here.
16 CARRIE: Famous last words.
17 HANNAH: Did I ever tell you about the time I was baby-sitting
18   and the little girl came to the top of the stairs crying, and
19   she was saying, "He's in my room! He's in my room!" My
20   heart was beating so fast. I wanted to run right out of
21   there. I think I would have, too, if someone had actually
22   come up behind her.
23 BRIDGET: So what happened? What was she talking about?
24 HANNAH: Turns out she was having a bad dream. But she
25   looked so scared. It really freaked me out. I just stood at
26   the bottom of the stairs and made her come to me — the
27   whole time my eyes were glued above her head, watching
28   to see if some psycho guy was going to appear behind her.
29 CARRIE: Omigosh! That is so scary!
30 HANNAH: I wouldn't take her back upstairs either. I called my
31   mom and made her come over until the parents got home.
32 BRIDGET: Chicken!
33 HANNAH: Yup. And proud of it! It's always scarier being in a
34   strange house anyway.
35 CARRIE: I know! You hear, like, every little noise!

1 HANNAH: The shadows are the worst! You'll see something out
2   of the corner of your eye and you just know it's an axe
3   murderer or something!
4 BRIDGET: Do you guys ever sleep when you're baby-sitting?
5 HANNAH: Not on purpose! But sometimes I doze off ... it just
6   gets too quiet after all the kids are in bed, you know?
7 CARRIE: One time I dozed off and the parents came home and
8   I didn't hear them — well, the mother put her hand on my
9   arm to wake me up and I started screaming bloody murder!
10   Woke all three of her kids up. She was *not* happy.
11 HANNAH: Well, that was totally her fault! You can't do that to
12   a person!
13 CARRIE: Yeah, and don't ever tell your brother you're baby-
14   sitting either. Jason thought it was funny one night to
15   scrape his fingers down the window while I was baby-
16   sitting. Of course it wasn't so funny when the cops came
17   because I called 9-1-1. Not only did the police lecture him,
18   but Mom and Dad grounded him for a month and made him
19   do my chores, too. It was almost worth getting scared half
20   to death.
21 BRIDGET: You think that's bad? My friend was mad because
22   she said I "stole" *(Air quotes)* her best family from her. Can
23   I help it that the kids liked me better than her? All she did
24   was talk on the phone all night. I actually played with
25   them! Anyway, to get even with me, she and a few of her
26   friends got one of those scary Halloween tapes —
27 HANNAH: You mean the ones with the howling and screaming?
28 BRIDGET: Exactly. They played it outside the window while a
29   few of them rattled the doorknobs and windows like they
30   were trying to get in.
31 CARRIE: That's horrible! You must have been terrified!
32 BRIDGET: Actually, no. They were pretty stupid. They didn't
33   even dress in black. Almost right away I spotted Erica in
34   one of our school sweatshirts. I knew it was her and her
35   friends the whole time. But I got even.

1 HANNAH: What'd you do?
2 BRIDGET: Well, this was a pretty expensive house with lots of
3   cool things. Like a sprinkler system you turned on from the
4   inside.
5 CARRIE: That's awesome!
6 BRIDGET: Yup! I soaked them all! It was beautiful. They ran out
7   of there like the wet, mangy dogs that they were!
8 HANNAH: Major payback!
9 BRIDGET: And they trampled Mrs. Hunt's flowers on the way
10   out. So when I told her what happened, she said she would
11   never use Erica ever again as a baby-sitter!
12 CARRIE: Double payback!
13 BRIDGET: You said it! Mrs. Hunt pays better than anyone, too.
14 HANNAH: Um ... whose house did you say this was?
15 BRIDGET: Very funny! You're not stealing my best gig! Even
16   better than the money is the premium ice cream she keeps
17   stocked in the freezer. It's totally amazing. One night I ate
18   a whole half-gallon!
19 HANNAH: Good! Keep it up. Maybe you'll eat yourself right out
20   of a job!
21 BRIDGET: I think they can afford it. The house is three stories
22   tall with a basement *and* an attic.
23 CARRIE: Ooooh. I don't do houses with attics. Too scary.
24 HANNAH: I don't mind the attic as much as basements. They're
25   way too dark and creepy.
26 BRIDGET: Scaredy cats! I'll tell you the creepiest room of the
27   house ... the bathroom!
28 HANNAH: Maybe after my brother's been in there awhile ...
29 CARRIE: The bathroom isn't scary! That's the first place I go
30   when something spooks me! I lock myself in there —
31 HANNAH: Sometimes I hide in the shower!
32 BRIDGET: Have you never even seen a horror movie? That's the
33   first place they always look! *(Pause)* But that's not what
34   makes the bathroom so scary.
35 CARRIE: Then what is it?

1 BRIDGET: The legend of Bloody Mary.
2 CARRIE: What happened to her? Was she hacked up in the
3   shower?
4 BRIDGET: No. It's far worse than that! See, she was this young
5   girl who died all of a sudden and her parents were so upset
6   — like they didn't really want to believe that their little girl
7   was dead! So they put this string in her coffin and they tied
8   it to a bell above the ground so that if she "woke up" she
9   could ring the bell and they could go get her.
10 HANNAH: Like dig her up? Like the chick's just going to calmly
11   wake up in a coffin and think to pull a string to ring a bell?
12 CARRIE: Really, I'd be screaming bloody murder if I woke up six
13   feet under!
14 BRIDGET: Well, the legend says that apparently the girl did
15   wake up. She pulled and pulled the string, only it was a
16   stormy night and no one heard the bell ringing. In
17   desperation, she pulled so hard, the bell ripped out of the
18   ground. The next day the mother went to the grave and
19   saw the bell lying on the ground and she went crazy!
20 CARRIE: That's horrible ... but what's that got to do with a
21   bathroom?
22 BRIDGET: I'm not sure about that part. All I know is this:
23   Whenever you stand in front of the bathroom mirror and
24   say "Bloody Mary" three times, you'll hear a bell ringing
25   and then you'll see Bloody Mary in the mirror behind you.
26 HANNAH: What? That's crazy!
27 CARRIE: Really. There's no way that's true.
28 BRIDGET: Well, that's the legend. They say if you see her face,
29   you'll go crazy like her mother.
30 HANNAH: I don't believe that for a minute.
31 BRIDGET: There's really only one way to find out.
32 HANNAH: Oh, come on. You don't expect us to really do it?
33 BRIDGET: I *dare* you to do it. Stand in front of the mirror, turn
34   and say "Bloody Mary" three times. If you're so sure it's
35   not true, what's the harm?

1   HANNAH: *(Obviously scared but not wanting to show it)* **Fine. I'll**
2   **do it. It's just a stupid scary story. Nobody actually**
3   **believes it.**
4   BRIDGET: Tell that to my friend's cousin's sister. She did it and
5   she's been locked up in the looney bin ever since.
6   HANNAH: Friend's cousin's sister? Isn't that who *all* the urban
7   legends happen to? It's never someone you actually know.
8   BRIDGET: Fine. It's your sanity, Hannah. Not mine.
9   CARRIE: I think you're crazy just for thinking about doing it! *(All*
10   *three girls move Offstage for a moment. HANNAH says "Bloody*
11   *Mary" three times and then gives a bloodcurdling scream. All*
12   *three run back On-stage.)*
13   BRIDGET: Did you see her? Did you see Bloody Mary?
14   CARRIE: Hannah! Are you OK?
15   HANNAH: *(Makes a crazy face and groans. Then she starts*
16   *laughing.)* **Omigosh! You should've seen your faces! You**
17   **were so freaked out when I started screaming!**
18   BRIDGET: I can't believe you did that! My heart is still
19   pounding! You got me good!
20   CARRIE: Me, too. I think I may have peed a little!
21   HANNAH: Priceless! I just have one question: where'd you get
22   that bloody mask from so fast? That was awesome!
23   *(BRIDGET and CARRIE's eyes widen as they look at each other.)*
24   BRIDGET and CARRIE: What bloody mask? *(All three look at*
25   *each other, terrified, and then scream.)*

The Student's View

(3 Girls, 1 Guy; Up to 5 Either)

CHARACTERS:

    Bob: Teenage boy who tends to be the peacemaker between Joy and Lisa.

    Joy: Loud-mouthed teenage girl who appears to be very excited about the show and the website they are talking about.

    Lisa: Very disbelieving and sarcastic. Likes to argue with Joy.

    Callers 1-5: Can be the same person who uses different voices/accents to play all parts, or can be several guys and girls.

    Chastity: Calls the hotline to clarify who broke up with whom.

SETTING:

    Sound room of a student radio show. Bob, Joy, and Lisa sitting around a table. Can have headsets on, if desired. A switchboard contraption can be placed in the middle of the table, as well as a microphone on a stand that they lean into to talk at times. All props are optional and can be omitted and pantomimed.

1 BOB: Hello, and welcome to *The Student's View.*
2 LISA: We've got a great show lined up for you today. As the
3 temperatures climb higher and higher, the heat is on
4 everyone's mind.
5 JOY: Hot date movie of the week: *Love and a Teenage Vampire.*
6 LISA: Our student reviews have given it a big thumbs up.
7 BOB: Here's what freshman Jamie Wilson has to say, "This
8 movie rocks. It's got something for the girls and the guys!
9 A little bit of romance and a whole lot of gore. It's the
10 perfect date movie!"
11 JOY: Senior Andy James says, "My date got so scared, she was
12 practically in my lap! This is definitely a must-see!"
13 BOB: Even the teachers love it. Mr. Johnson says, "My daughter
14 drug me to this movie and I thought I'd hate every minute.
15 But, in all actuality, it wasn't half-bad."
16 LISA: An endorsement from Mr. Johnson? This definitely
17 sounds like one movie you won't want to miss!
18 BOB: Next in hot topics: Prom King and Queen no longer a
19 couple! That's right! You heard it here first! Question is:
20 Who dumped whom?
21 JOY: Our sources tell us Chastity Graves was seen dining with
22 Jimmy Harris at the Pizza Palace on Friday night. Sounds
23 like maybe Chastity broke Mr. Prom King's heart.
24 LISA: This just in: A friend of Jordan Smith's, notorious Prom
25 King, says that Jordan was seen holding hands with a yet-
26 to-be-named girl the very same night. Maybe Jordan wasn't
27 the dumpee after all.
28 BOB: If anyone has information on this hot topic, please call the
29 hotline.
30 LISA: In other hot school news: We've got twenty subs in the
31 building today. Looks like students aren't the only ones
32 with senioritis!
33 JOY: Mysterious teacher illness? Or the fact that we've only got
34 ten more days of school?
35 BOB: But the end of the school year isn't what's on our minds

1   today. Today we'll be talking about how you'll be spending
2   eternity.
3   JOY: Grab a pen and write this down: www-dot-Get-You-a-Spot-
4   in-Heaven-dot-com. Trust me, you're going to want to
5   check this out!
6   BOB: Mr. Shelton's trig class is the best place to sneak online!
7   J-K, Mr. Shelton! You're class is totally *not* boring!
8   JOY: You just got yourself a solid F in there, Bob!
9   LISA: Let's get back to the website. Get you a spot in heaven?
10   Are you kidding me?
11   BOB: No! It's completely real. I checked it out. They even take
12   credit cards!
13   LISA: That doesn't make it real, Bob. That just makes it a
14   scam that's out to get your money.
15   JOY: Look. They take Paypal, too. I'm pretty sure Paypal makes
16   sure it's a valid site.
17   LISA: *(Disbelieving)* You two really believe this website is going
18   to tell us how we can get a spot in heaven? This is the
19   most ridiculous thing I've ever heard.
20   JOY: This is awesome! We're going to give students a direct line
21   to heaven.
22   BOB: And who needs that more than us? I don't know about
23   you but I sure would like a guarantee.
24   JOY: Who wouldn't? This is like a free pass into heaven! It
25   completely rocks!
26   LISA: Well, of course that would appeal to you.
27   JOY: What do you mean by that?
28   LISA: If there's an easy way to do things, you always want it.
29   JOY: Who doesn't?
30   LISA: People like me, who know some things can't be had just
31   like that. *(Snaps.)* Some things you have to work for, you
32   know?
33   BOB: Why would we? Listen to this: "At Get You a Spot in
34   Heaven we offer you a one-hundred-percent-guaranteed
35   spot in heaven."

1   LISA: *(Sarcastically and laughing)* **Well,** it's not like you'll be
2   around to get your money back. They kind of got you there.
3   JOY: Never mind her, folks. She's always cranky early in the
4   morning. Probably because she has to get up three hours
5   early just to get her hair that straight.
6   LISA: At least I fix my hair. You look like you just rolled out of
7   bed. Good thing this is a radio show, Joy, or you might get
8   fired.
9   JOY: It's really good that it's radio, Lisa, because you sure
10   couldn't stand another ten pounds the camera would add!
11   BOB: Girls! Let's get back on track here. Look, we have a caller.
12   LISA: *(Acts like she's flipping on a switch.)* **Hello.** You're on *The*
13   *Student's View.* Do you have a question for us?
14   CALLER 1: I am the hand holder of Jordan Smith and I just
15   want to say that I know for a fact that *he* broke up with
16   that two-timing bleach blonde Chastity. He told me the
17   whole story the other night.
18   JOY: Excellent! Care to reveal your identity to all of our callers?
19   *(Pause)*
20   LISA: And it looks like we just lost our caller. Guess she wants
21   to remain anonymous.
22   BOB: Back to our story. We have another caller on the line.
23   CALLER 2: Yes! Can I reserve a spot for a friend or a family
24   member?
25   LISA: Oh, you've got to be kidding me! Do you think it's like a
26   restaurant or something?
27   JOY: *(Leaning into mic to talk to caller)* **Great** question! It says
28   right here that they absolutely encourage you to reserve a
29   spot for a friend or loved one ...
30   LISA: Of course they do.
31   JOY: ... When you are on the checkout page just remember to
32   put the name — spelled out exactly as you want — in the
33   correct areas.
34   CALLER 2: Thanks! I'll do that! This will make a great present
35   for all my friends and family!

1   BOB: Then you'll love this! They offer group discounts for five or
2   more people.
3   JOY: They offer discounts, Lisa. That should make you happy.
4   We all know how you love a good bargain.
5   LISA: Are you calling me cheap, Joy?
6   JOY: I believe you called me lazy.
7   LISA: And I believe you called me fat.
8   JOY: Well, if the shoe fits ...
9   BOB: *(Interrupting)* Thanks for calling! Looks like we have
10   another caller on the line. *(Pretends to flip switch.)* Hello and
11   welcome to *The Student's View.* Do you have a question
12   today?
13 CHASTITY: No, I don't have a question. I have a comment. This
14   is Chastity Graves and I'd like to tell everyone the truth
15   about what happened! Of course Jordan would want
16   everyone to think that I cheated on him. But the truth is,
17   the reason why Susan Holmes — that's right I blew your
18   cover Susan — wants to remain anonymous is because
19   she's the one who stole Jordan from *me!* He's the two-
20   timing jerk — not me!
21 LISA: Well, thank you Chastity for clearing that up for us. You
22   heard it straight from the source folks!
23 BOB: Back to our callers. We've got one holding now.
24 CALLER 3: Who cares about Jordan, Susan, or Chastity? I'm
25   worried about my pets! Can I get a spot for them? I can't
26   imagine leaving my cats behind!
27 JOY: Oh no! Me either! I'd have to take my dogs, Brewster and
28   Spot, with me!
29 BOB: Good news for you both! If you would like your pets to join
30   you in heaven then you can reserve their spot also. It's the
31   only way to know for sure that they will be joining you in
32   the afterlife.
33 CALLER 3: That is awesome!
34 JOY: You said it, caller! What is your pet's name?
35 CALLER 3: I have a tarantula named Spike.

1 JOY: Weird. But OK! I guess heaven has space for eight-legged
2   freaks, too.
3 LISA: Call me weird, but I'm thinking spiders are definitely *not*
4   making it into heaven.
5 JOY: Well, it's a good thing that you're not heading up the pearly
6   gates then. I know I will definitely be getting a reservation
7   for my dogs.
8 LISA: *(Extremely sarcastically)* I'm sure there's a special doggy
9   park for them to run and play in, too!
10 JOY: Well, of course none of us knows for sure what heaven will
11   be like.
12 LISA: So this site is selling one-way tickets to a place no one's
13   even seen? Never visited? Buyers beware! Sounds like
14   swampland in Florida to me.
15 JOY: Call me stupid but I'm pretty sure that heaven does exist.
16 LISA: OK, stupid. That's not the point. Of course it exists!
17 JOY: Then what is the problem again?
18 LISA: *(Deep sigh)* Look. Everyone knows there is only one way
19   to get into heaven. And this is *not* it.
20 JOY: You're so closed-minded, Lisa. You never believe in
21   anything.
22 LISA: Just because I know better than to buy into a scam like
23   this doesn't mean I'm closed-minded.
24 JOY: You just can't accept that there might be a way other than
25   *your way* to get to heaven.
26 LISA: Yeah, well, only a moron would fall for something
27   ridiculous like this.
28 BOB: Girls! Let's get back on track here. We need to tell our
29   listeners what the first step to getting a reservation is.
30 JOY: What is the first step?
31 BOB: First you need to decide if you want a standard
32   reservation or a luxury reservation.
33 LISA: You've got to be kidding me!
34 JOY: *(Ignoring LISA)* So what's the difference between the two?
35 BOB: Well, I read all about it earlier and it sounds like the

1   standard reservation is your basic package. Nothing fancy.
2   The luxury reservation makes sure that you're surrounded
3   by high-moral-caliber people. You know, the minimal
4   sinners. No murderers or rapists allowed. Not even the
5   converted ones. It's basically where all the elite get
6   together.
7 JOY: Sounds like my kind of place! You never know who you
8   might get stuck with if you go with the standard
9   reservation.
10 BOB: Yeah, I'm thinking you might not want to take any
11   chances. You never know what kind of people are going to
12   make it up there.
13 LISA: Come on! Do you really think heaven is going to have
14   upper and middle classes? That you can just buy your way
15   into heaven and then pick who you get to hang around?
16   *(Leans into JOY.)* Oh, sad for you then, Joy. You won't see
17   half your friends there!
18 JOY: What are you trying to say, Lisa? That my friends aren't
19   high moral caliber?
20 LISA: I doubt your friends even know what that means!
21 JOY: Obviously, since I used to think that you were my friend!
22 BOB: *(Obviously breaking things up again)* Look! We have another
23   caller! *(Flips switch.)* Hello and welcome to *The Student's*
24   *View.* Do you have a question for us?
25 CALLER 4: Yeah. I guess I'm wondering *why* we should reserve
26   a spot. Can't we just take our chances? See if we get in?
27 JOY: Oh no! The website is very clear about that!
28 BOB: That's right! At the moment there is plenty of room in
29   Heaven, but spots are filling very quickly. So quick that if
30   you don't act now you may lose your chance at getting in.
31 JOY: That's awful! How does a future of endless suffering
32   sound? Not so good, which is why Get You a Spot in
33   Heaven is there to help.
34 BOB: Looks like we have time for one more caller.
35 JOY: *(Flipping on a switch)* Hello and welcome to *The Student's*

1   *View.* Do you have a question?

2 CALLER 5: Yes. Can you tell me how much the luxury
3   reservation costs?

4 BOB: The luxury reservation is twenty-nine ninety-five, and the
5   standard reservation is nineteen ninety-five.

6 JOY: They both come with a certificate suitable for framing, a
7   key chain, and if you act now, they're offering buy one get
8   one free!

9 CALLER 5: Wow. Twenty-nine ninety-five. That seems a little
10   steep.

11 BOB: True. But who can put a price on eternity?

12 LISA: Well, apparently Get You a Spot in Heaven can.

13 JOY: OK ... well, I think that's all the time we have today.

14 BOB: Thanks for taking the time to listen to ...

15 ALL 3: *The Student's View.*

16 JOY: Be sure and join us tomorrow as we discuss summer
17   vacation options!

18 BOB: Don't forget, we want to hear from you! E-mail us your
19   summer vacation plans and we'll be sure to put them on
20   the air!

21 LISA: And that's a wrap.

22 BOB: That was one of our best shows yet!

23 JOY: Really. Can you believe the callers? They actually bought
24   that stuff! Completely amazing.

25 LISA: I know! For a moment there, I thought you did, too. Great
26   acting, by the way!

27 BOB: Yeah, I especially loved the part about Brewster and Spot!

28 JOY: Could you believe that girl asking if she could reserve a
29   spot for her *tarantula*? What a complete moron!

30 LISA: What about the girl who's going to buy all of her friends
31   and family into heaven? Can you say pathetic?

32 BOB: Uh ... guys ... why is the recording light still on?

33 JOY: I thought you said we were off the air!

34 ALL 3: *Oh no!*

Talk to a Star

(4 Girls)
CHARACTERS:

Operator: This is a "taped recording" so the operator should sound canned.

Kate: Teenage girl who is starstruck and gets frustrated trying to get through to her favorite star.

Sandi: Kate's friend.

Kate's Mom: Has something important to tell Kate.

SETTING:

Kate is Center Stage on the phone. Operator is Stage Right on phone. They do not look at each other throughout the skit, as if they are not in same room. Later, when Sandi is on the phone, she will be Stage Left.

1 OPERATOR: Hello and welcome to the newly automated Talk
2   Directly to a Star Network. If you know the name of the
3   star you would like to speak to, please say "one."
4 KATE: One.
5 OPERATOR: I'm sorry. That is not a valid selection. If you know
6   the name of the star you would like to speak to, please —
7 KATE: *One!*
8 OPERATOR: You've reached a department that is currently
9   closed. If you'd like to go back to the main menu, please
10   say "zero." To hear the directory, please say "two." To talk
11   to a star, please say "three."
12 KATE: Three.
13 OPERATOR: I'm sorry. You have selected an incorrect option. To
14   hear the selections again, please say "one."
15 KATE: Three. I mean, one. *One!*
16 OPERATOR: I'm sorry. You can only choose one option at a
17   time. To return to the main menu, please say "zero."
18 KATE: Zero.
19 OPERATOR: Hablar en Español, por favor.
20 KATE: Oh, come on!
21 OPERATOR: No comprendo. Si habla Español, diga "uno." Para
22   engles, diga "dos."
23 KATE: Dos! Dos!
24 OPERATOR: I'm sorry. I did not understand your selection.
25   Please say "zero" to return to the main menu. If you know
26   the name of the star you would like to speak to, say the
27   name clearly into the phone.
28 KATE: What? Why didn't you say that before?
29 OPERATOR: I'm sorry. We do not have a star by that name. To
30   hear the directory, please say "two."
31 KATE: Two!
32 OPERATOR: You've reached the directory of the Talk to a Star
33   Network.
34 KATE: Finally!
35 OPERATOR: I'm sorry. "Finally" is not a valid star selection. To

1   hear your options again, please say "zero." To return to the
2   directory, please say "two." If you know the name of your
3   star, please say "three."
4 KATE: Three! Three! Three! For crying out loud, three!
5 OPERATOR: Your selection was three. If this is correct, please
6   say yes.
7 KATE: Yes!
8 OPERATOR: Please speak the name of the star you wish to
9   speak to clearly into the phone.
10 KATE: Brad Pitt.
11 OPERATOR: You have selected Mark Spitz. If this is correct, say
12   "yes." If not, say "no."
13 KATE: No!
14 OPERATOR: To which star would you like to speak?
15 KATE: Brad Pitt!
16 OPERATOR: You have selected Brad Pitt. If this is correct,
17   please say "yes."
18 KATE: Yes!
19 OPERATOR: Please hold while we connect you to Brad Pitt. We
20   appreciate your patience while we get Mr. Pitt on the line
21   for you.
22 KATE: Omigosh! This is so exciting! I'm actually going to talk
23   to Brad Pitt. For real. Right now. Me. Him. This is too
24   good. *(Pause)* I've got to three-way Sandi in on this. *(Pulls*
25   *phone from ear and starts pushing buttons, as she's putting it*
26   *back to her ear, she says, "Sandi?")*
27 OPERATOR: Welcome to the main directory of the Talk Directly
28   to a Star Network. To hear the directory of stars, please
29   say one.
30 KATE: *Noooo!*
31 OPERATOR: I'm sorry. That is not a valid selection.
32 SANDI: Hello? Hello? Who is this?
33 KATE: *(Puts phone back up to ear.)* Sandi?
34 SANDI: Kate?
35 KATE: Yeah. It's me.

1 OPERATOR: *(For the remaining call, the OPERATOR will interject*
2 *comments into their conversation. They will talk over her when*
3 *possible.)* **If you would like to speak —**
4 SANDI: Who is that on the line with us?
5 KATE: *(Frustrated)* It's the operator from Talk Directly to a Star
6 Network.
7 SANDI: OK. I'll bite. Why is the operator from Talk Directly to a
8 Star Network on our phone call?
9 OPERATOR: I'm sorry that is not a valid selection. Please hold
10 while we transfer you to the main directory.
11 KATE: I was trying to get you, me, and Brad Pitt on the phone
12 together.
13 SANDI: Kate, tell me that you didn't fall for that!
14 KATE: It's real! I got the number out of the back of my
15 magazine.
16 SANDI: Kate! My cousin did that once and his phone bill was
17 something like four-hundred dollars!
18 KATE: No way! Where'd he call, Japan?
19 SANDI: No. It was some eight-eight-eight number. The worst
20 part is, he never even got to talk to a star. He was caught
21 in some kind of phone loop ...
22 OPERATOR: Please speak the name of the star you wish to
23 speak to, clearly into the phone.
24 KATE: That's what happened to me and just when he was
25 supposed to get on the line, I lost him!
26 SANDI: That's what happened to Tim! His parents were so mad;
27 they took his cell phone for over a year!
28 KATE: My parents would kill me first and ask questions later!
29 SANDI: Did the operator say how much this was going to cost
30 you?
31 OPERATOR: I'm sorry. That is not a valid star name. If you
32 would like to hear the directory of stars, please press —
33 KATE: Well, it's not as bad as your cousin's. This is only four-
34 ninety-nine a call.
35 SANDI: A call? Are you sure? I think my cousin paid four-ninety-

1   nine a *minute!*
2   KATE: A minute?! No way! They can't charge that much for a
3   stupid phone call.
4   SANDI: Do you still have the magazine? Look it up!
5   OPERATOR: I'm sorry that is not a valid selection —
6   SANDI: Quick!
7   KATE: *(Flips through the magazine frantically, then squints and*
8   *holds it closer while she reads the fine print.)* Omigosh.
9   Omigosh. *Omigosh!* Sandi, it's four-ninety-nine a *minute!* I
10   am so dead! I am *so so dead!*
11 SANDI: You've got to get rid of her! Now!
12 KATE: Yeah, you're right! Hold on! *(Holds phone out and starts*
13   *pushing buttons. Then puts phone back to ear.)* Hello?
14 SANDI: I'm still here.
15 KATE: Oh, thank goodness. I think I —
16 OPERATOR: I'm sorry. You've reached a department —
17 KATE: Aaaahhhh! What do I do? What do I do?
18 SANDI: Hang up the phone, Kate! *Hang up the phone! (KATE*
19   *hangs up the phone and throws it across the room. She stares*
20   *at it for a second as if she's afraid of it. MOM enters her room.)*
21 MOM: Hey, honey. What are you up to?
22 KATE: *(Very defensive and nervous)* Nothing. Why? What do you
23   mean? What do you think I've been doing? Geez, you
24   always think I'm up to something.
25 MOM: *(Taken aback)* No. I didn't mean ... *(Pause)* I just came up
26   here to talk to you.
27 KATE: Oh. *(Trying to regain composure from feeling guilty)* OK.
28   What did you want to talk about?
29 MOM: *(Looks around nervously like she's not sure how to tell her*
30   *this.)* I don't really know where to start ... so I guess I'll just
31   have to jump in.
32 KATE: What are you talking about? Is something wrong?
33 MOM: *(Takes KATE's hand.)* Kate, honey. Your dad isn't on a
34   business trip.
35 KATE: What? Yes he is. I just talked to him yesterday. He called

1   from San Diego. He said the weather is beautiful.

2 MOM: *(Sadly)* I know that's what he said. But he's not in San
3   Diego, Kate.

4 KATE: Why would he lie? Why are you telling me this? It doesn't
5   make any sense. You told me he was on business.
6   Remember?

7 MOM: I know. I'm sorry. I shouldn't have lied. It just happened
8   so quickly and we didn't know what to say to you.

9 KATE: What happened so quickly? Mom, you're scaring me. Tell
10   me what's going on.

11 MOM: *(Deep breath)* Your dad moved out. He's not coming back.

12 KATE: What do you mean "he's not coming back"? Of course
13   he's coming back. He told me he'll be home on Friday.
14   That's only two more days. *(Starting to get hysterical)*

15 MOM: *(Firmly)* Kate. He's not coming back. Not here at least.

16 KATE: Then where is he? If he's not in San Diego, where the
17   heck is he?

18 MOM: He's staying with a friend a few miles away.

19 KATE: A friend? My dad's supposedly been gone for over two
20   weeks on business and he's just been down the road at *a*
21   *friend's*?

22 MOM: I know it's hard to understand.

23 KATE: Of course it's hard to understand. My own father doesn't
24   even want to see me!

25 MOM: No. It's not like that. Of course he wants to see you. We
26   just needed some distance for a little bit.

27 KATE: No! *You* needed distance! Not me! Not him! Why did he
28   have to be distant from me?

29 MOM: We just weren't ready to tell you. We had to be sure this
30   is what we both wanted.

31 KATE: What about me? What about what I want? Doesn't that
32   matter?

33 MOM: Of course it does. But Kate, this is a problem between
34   your dad and me. It has nothing to do with you.

35 KATE: Really? *Really*, Mom? Nothing to do with me? Are you

1   serious?
2 MOM: I didn't mean it that way. Of course it's going to affect
3   you. I'm sorry about that. But the problem isn't you. You
4   have to know that we've tried to fix things for a long time.
5   They just don't seem to stay fixed.
6 KATE: Then try a little harder. You guys can't get divorced.
7 MOM: We're not getting divorced. We're just going to live apart
8   for a while.
9 KATE: I wasn't born yesterday, Mom. A lot of my friends have
10   already gone through this. I know how it works. Once you
11   separate, there's no going back.
12 MOM: *(Looks down for a second then up at Kate.)* You're probably
13   right. Sometimes you just know when it's over. You don't
14   want it to be, but you know it is.
15 KATE: *(Tearful)* Then it's over? It's really over?
16 MOM: Yes, honey, it is.
17 KATE: So he's never coming back? I'll never see him at the
18   table? Never see him working in the garage? Never?
19 MOM: I'm afraid not. He's coming to get the rest of his things
20   this weekend. And, of course, he wants to see you. He's
21   going to get a place of his own so that you'll have
22   someplace to stay when you visit him.
23 KATE: Visit him? Like a guest?
24 MOM: No. Like his daughter.
25 KATE: I don't think it's going to feel that way, Mom. For some
26   reason, I don't think it's ever going to feel right again.
27 MOM: It's going to be OK. *(Hugs her.)* I'm sorry I lied to you.
28   You're so important to me, and I love you so much. I don't
29   ever want there to be lies between us Kate.
30 KATE: *(Looks at the phone lying across the room.)* Mom ... there's
31   something I need to tell you.

Jealousy

(3 Girls, 2 Guys, 1 Walk-on with no lines)
CHARACTERS:

Sara: Very giving girl who, for no reason at all, buys her friends gifts just to show them that she's thinking about them.

Trish: Girl who loves her gift ... until she sees that everyone else's gift is bigger and better. She thinks bigger means that Sara cares more for them than for her.

Ben: Guy who gets one of Sara's gifts.

Emma: Girl who gets one of Sara's gifts.

Jack: Guy who gets one of Sara's gifts. Jack is a dramatic, outgoing guy. He says things like "Girrrrl, you are craaaazy!"

Student: Guy or girl who may also have gotten one of Sara's gifts.

SETTING:

Somewhere at school. The specific room or hallway doesn't matter.

1 *(TRISH is On-stage. SARA walks on.)*
2 **SARA: Hey, Trish. I've been looking for you. I got you**
3   **something.**
4 **TRISH: For me? Really? How sweet! Why?**
5 **SARA: No reason. I saw it and I thought of you.** *(Hands her a key*
6   *chain with a mini notebook on it – this can be real or imagined.)*
7 **TRISH: Wow! This is so cool. A mini-notebook key chain!**
8 **SARA: Yeah I knew you liked tiny cutesy things.**
9 **TRISH: Oh, it really is cute. I mean look at it. It's perfect!**
10   **Thanks!**
11 **SARA: No problem. I'm glad you like it.**
12 **TRISH: Like it? I** *love* **it! It is so adorable.**
13 **SARA: Well, I gotta run. I'll see you later.**
14 **TRISH: OK. Thanks again! That was really sweet of you!** *(TRISH*
15   *sits back down, and in comes BEN.)*
16 **BEN: You're looking awfully happy.**
17 **TRISH: I am. Look. Isn't this cute?**
18 **BEN: Eh, I guess. Where did you get it?**
19 **TRISH: Sara got it for me. Wasn't that thoughtful? She said it**
20   **reminded her of me and so she got it. For no reason at all.**
21   **She is so considerate.**
22 **BEN: Cool.** *(He digs in his backpack and pulls out a journal-size*
23   *notebook. TRISH looks from her mini notebook to BEN's journal-*
24   *sized notebook and then back at hers. She is obviously*
25   *disappointed.)*
26 **TRISH: Wow. That's a pretty cool journal you've got there.**
27 **BEN: This? Yeah, it's all right.**
28 **TRISH: All right? Why, it's twice the size of mine.**
29 **BEN: I know. I like to write a lot.**
30 **TRISH: Yeah. Me too.** *(Bummed)* **So where'd you get it?**
31 **BEN: Sara.**
32 **TRISH: Really? Sara gave that to you?**
33 **BEN: Uh-huh.**
34 **TRISH: Why? Why'd she give you that?**
35 **BEN:** *(Shrugs.)* **No reason. Just gave it to me.**

1 TRISH: *(Clearly upset)* **Huh. Well. That was nice of her.**

2 BEN: **Yeah. Like you said. She's pretty considerate. Always**
3 **thinking of others.**

4 TRISH: *(Sarcastically)* **Practically a saint.**

5 BEN: **Well, I gotta go. See ya later.** *(TRISH is left sitting there*
6 *looking at her mini notebook, not quite as enthusiastic as she*
7 *was a moment ago. In walks EMMA.)*

8 EMMA: **Hey, Trish. What're you doing?**

9 TRISH: **Nothing much. Just sitting here.** *(EMMA sits down next*
10 *to her.)*

11 EMMA: **Cool key chain.**

12 TRISH: *(Looks at it, half-way excited again.)* **Yeah. It is kinda cool,**
13 **isn't it? It's got this baby notebook attached to it.**

14 EMMA: **I see. That's really neat.** *(Digs in backpack and takes out*
15 *a full-sized one-subject notebook.)*

16 TRISH: **Wow! That's awesome.**

17 EMMA: **I know! It's glittery purple and everything. You know**
18 **purple is my favorite color.**

19 TRISH: **Yeah.** *(Pause)* **I like purple, too.**

20 EMMA: **Best part is, it's got two-hundred and fifty pages. I**
21 **definitely need that 'cause I write really big.**

22 TRISH: **That's true.** *(Holds up her mini key chain.)* **You probably**
23 **couldn't even begin to write in something this small.**

24 EMMA: **Not a chance. I doubt I could even fit my name on a**
25 **page that tiny! Good thing you write small.**

26 TRISH: *(Sulking)* **Well, I don't write** *that* **small.**

27 EMMA: **Yes, you do. The teacher practically has to have a**
28 **magnifying glass to read your writing.**

29 TRISH: **Funny. So where'd you get that big fancy purple**
30 **notebook anyway?**

31 EMMA: **Sara.**

32 TRISH: **Sara? Really? Sara gave you that?**

33 EMMA: **Uh-huh.**

34 TRISH: **Wow. That's really nice.**

35 EMMA: **Yeah. I was pretty psyched to get it.**

1   TRISH: So why'd she give you that?

2   EMMA: *(Shrugs.)* I don't know. Just did. Guess she remembered

3   I like purple. She's pretty thoughtful that way.

4   TRISH: *(Depressed again)* Yeah. She's thoughtful all right.

5   EMMA: Well, I gotta go. I already wrote a story in here for

6   English class and I need to go type it up. See you later!

7   TRISH: *(Under her breath)* Pssssh. I probably couldn't even write

8   the title of a story in this stupid thing. *(TRISH is very*

9   *dejected now, rolling eyes and everything. In comes JACK.)*

10 JACK: Hey.

11 TRISH: *(Very sullen.)* Hey.

12 JACK: What's the matter?

13 TRISH: Oh. Nothing. Just looking at this stupid key chain.

14 JACK: Stupid? Let me see? *(Pause, then very dramatic)* Why, I

15   think that's the cutest thing I've ever seen!

16 TRISH: *(Perks back up.)* Really? You think so?

17 JACK: *Girrrrl!* It's adorable!

18 TRISH: *(Even more excited.)* It is pretty neat. *(JACK digs in bag,*

19   *pulls out a very thick three-subject notebook.)*

20 TRISH: *(Overdramatic shock)* What is *that?*

21 JACK: Oh, just a notebook.

22 TRISH: "Just a notebook"?! That thing has three sections! How

23   many pages is it, anyway? A million?!

24 JACK: *(Sarcastically)* Yeah. It's a million pages, Trish. They make

25   those, you know.

26 TRISH: OK. I was exaggerating. Obviously. So how many does

27   it have?

28 JACK: *(Looks at the cover.)* Well, it's a whole lot less than a

29   million. It's only got a thousand pages.

30 TRISH: *(Obviously overly upset)* Only a thousand? *Only* a

31   thousand! Are you kidding me?

32 JACK: Why would I kid about something like that? Are you OK?

33   I mean, seriously, it's a notebook.

34 TRISH: Maybe to you. To me, it's a whole lot more. I mean, look

35   at this! *(Pointing from her mini notebook to JACK's big*

1   *notebook)* I could put all the pages together and it wouldn't
2   even equal a page in that thing!
3 JACK: You're right. Mine is kind of big.
4 TRISH: Kind of? Come on, it's humongous!
5 JACK: *(Pacifying TRISH)* OK, it's humongous. Whatever. Do you
6   need a pill or something? *(Looks at her very strangely.)*
7 TRISH: *(Getting more and more upset)* Look at that! And then look
8   at this! *(Thrusting mini key chain in his face)* There's, like, no
9   comparison!
10 JACK: *(Pause — clearly doesn't know what to say.)* Well, yours is
11   still pretty cute.
12 TRISH: Yeah, if you're, like, three!
13 JACK: But it's perfect for you!
14 TRISH: Why? Because you think I'm not good enough to get a
15   big fancy three-subject notebook like you?
16 JACK: No, because you like little tiny things! Like the magnets
17   you're always collecting!
18 TRISH: Yeah. Whatever. Easy for you to say with your big jumbo
19   notebook. So where'd you get it anyhow? The jolly green
20   giant?
21 JACK: Funny. I got it from Sara.
22 TRISH: Sara? *My* Sara? You've got to be kidding me! She gave
23   you that! And me *this*?
24 JACK: *(Clearly thinks TRISH is crazy and wants to get out of there.)*
25   Yeah ... well ... I gotta go. See you later. *(SARA walks in as
26   JACK walks off. TRISH thrusts key chain back at SARA.)*
27 TRISH: Here. You can have it back.
28 SARA: What?
29 TRISH: I said you can have it back. I don't want it anymore.
30 SARA: Why? I thought you liked it.
31 TRISH: Well, I did ... at first. I mean, it was perfect. All cute and
32   little and all. But ... I thought you were my friend, Sara.
33   Like my *best* friend.
34 SARA: I am! That's why I got this for you. When I saw it, I
35   thought of you.

1   TRISH: Yeah, yeah, yeah ... it reminded you of me ... whatever
2   ... You gave me the smallest one! Everyone else got a
3   bigger one! And Jack's had three subjects! Three subjects
4   and a thousand pages! Why couldn't you give me one with
5   three subjects?
6   SARA: Because I picked this one just for you.
7   TRISH: But why? Why didn't you pick the big jumbo-sized one
8   for me? Don't you see how that made me feel? You got
9   everyone else something better than what you got me.
10 SARA: I'm sorry. I guess I didn't see it that way. Would it make
11   you happy if I gave you a big, jumbo-sized notebook
12   instead?
13 TRISH: Yes! Because then I would know for sure that you're
14   really *my* best friend. That you really care about me. Then
15   I wouldn't have the little itty-bitty notebook ...
16 SARA: The one that's perfect for you ...
17 TRISH: I would have the great, big three-subject notebook!
18 SARA: OK. If you're sure that's what you want. *(Digs in*
19   *backpack and hands TRISH a big three-subject notebook.)*
20 TRISH: *(Takes it and hugs her.)* Oh, thank you! Thank you! This
21   is so much better! I love it! Thank you!
22 SARA: Great. I'm glad you're happy now. I'll see you later.
23   *(SARA exits. TRISH sits back down and looks lovingly at her*
24   *big, jumbo-sized notebook. She is obviously pleased with herself*
25   *and how things have worked out. In walks another STUDENT*
26   *carrying a five-subject notebook that's obviously thicker than*
27   *TRISH's. The STUDENT crosses the stage. TRISH watches with a*
28   *shocked look.)*
29 TRISH: Hey, wait up! Where did you get that? *(Chases after the*
30   *STUDENT.)*

Sleepover

(4 Girls)

CHARACTERS:

Ashley, Gilly, and **Karen:** Self-absorbed, really into fashion and getting their hair and nails done; money is no object; obviously spoiled.

Tina: Saving money to sponsor a kid; doesn't think they should be spending so much money on clothes, hair, nails, etc.

SETTING:

At one of the girls' houses (not Tina's) for a sleepover. Girls are in pajamas, doing each other's hair, painting nails, etc.

1 ASHLEY: Did you guys see the new Hollister catalog?
2 GILLY: Yeah! I got it the day it came out. I've picked out at least
3   six shirts I've got to have before school starts.
4 KAREN: There's a skirt on page six that I'm getting as soon as
5   mom gives me this week's allowance.
6 TINA: Another skirt? You've got like a hundred already!
7 KAREN: *(She flips through the magazine to find the page, and then*
8   *shows it to everyone.)* Yeah, but this one is awesome! It's
9   pink *and* green! My two favorite colors!
10 ASHLEY: Ooooh! Did you see that fabulous dress on page
11   nineteen? I have got to convince my mom to let me buy
12   that!
13 KAREN: *(Flips to that page in the magazine.)* That is pretty. It
14   would look great on you!
15 ASHLEY: I know! That's why I just *have* to get it!
16 KAREN: Tell your mom you'll wear it to everything!
17 ASHLEY: I'd tell her I'd sleep in it, if that would help. But she's
18   going to flip at the price. She still thinks I should be able
19   to get a whole outfit for fifty dollars — and that's including
20   shoes and purse!
21 GILLY: She'd freak then if she knew this little gem *(holding up*
22   *her purse)* cost over a hundred dollars!
23 TINA: *I'm* freaking that you spent over a hundred dollars on a
24   purse!
25 KAREN: *(Holding up magazine and pointing)* And at seventy-nine
26   ninety-nine, I think you can kiss this dress good-bye!
27 ASHLEY: Yeah. *(Clearly bummed out)* I guess I'll have to wait for
28   it to go on clearance. And then it will be out of season!
29 GILLY: So why catalog shop? We should go to the mall tomorrow
30   and do some real shopping!
31 ASHLEY: And get our nails done!
32 KAREN: That'd be awesome! It's been almost a month since I
33   got my last manicure. *(Holding out hands to inspect them)*
34   They're really starting to look ratty. *(Shows them to*
35   *everyone.)*

1 GILLY: It's set. We'll go shopping, do our nails, and then go to
2   lunch. There's that new restaurant downtown that I heard
3   has killer salads!
4 TINA: The one with the valet parking? I bet it's pretty expensive.
5 KAREN: But so worth it!
6 ASHLEY: Yeah. We can splurge a little.
7 TINA: But I already ate out twice this week.
8 ASHLEY: Twice? That's nothing! I haven't had a meal at home
9   in over two weeks!
10 GILLY: That's what summer is for. Eating out and seeing
11   movies!
12 KAREN: Really. I've seen every movie at the theatre! I'm just
13   waiting to see what they release this week.
14 ASHLEY: I would kill to see a Matthew McConaughey movie
15   right now!
16 GILLY: I know! Did you see the one where he had his shirt off
17   for like half the movie? So hot!
18 KAREN: I'd even settle for one where he actually keeps his
19   clothes on!
20 GILLY: For real! No guy should look that stinking good!
21 ASHLEY: We should go to the movies, too! You know, end the
22   day that way!
23 TINA: A movie, too? Isn't that a little much?
24 KAREN: Nah. Why not make a total day and night of it? It's not
25   like any of us have boyfriends to run home to.
26 ASHLEY: Thanks for reminding us, Karen. Now we sound
27   pathetic.
28 KAREN: Boys. Who needs them?
29 GILLY, TINA, and ASHLEY: Us! *(Look at each other and laugh.)*
30 KAREN: OK. I'll give you that. But since we don't have them,
31   we might as well have some quality girl time!
32 GILLY: Sounds like chick flick time!
33 KAREN: There's that one about a girl getting married and her
34   best friend steals her boyfriend from her right before the
35   wedding.

1   ASHLEY: Same old, same old. But I'm game.

2   KAREN: Cool. We'll go to the mall, then get our nails done, grab

3   some lunch, and then see a movie! It'll be the best day!

4   ASHLEY: Sounds like a plan to me!

5   TINA: That sounds awesome, guys. But I think I'm going to

6   have to pass. I just don't have a lot of money right now.

7   ASHLEY: No problem. I can loan you some. My dad gives me

8   ridiculous amounts of money — you know, guilt money

9   over leaving my mom. But whatever. It works for me.

10   *(Reaches in purse to grab her wallet.)*

11 KAREN: Besides, that's what friends are for. We'll spot you.

12   *(She pulls out a credit card.)* That's what this little baby is

13   for. Emergency money!

14 TINA: This is hardly an emergency.

15 KAREN: A friend in need is always an emergency in my book!

16 TINA: Seriously. I'd love to but I can't. I have to watch what I'm

17   spending my money on.

18 ASHLEY: Why? You're the only one of us with a job! You should

19   have all kinds of money!

20 TINA: *(Sarcastically)* Yeah, my minimum wage job has me rolling

21   in the cash.

22 ASHLEY: You know what I mean. You don't even have to wait

23   on an allowance or anything.

24 TINA: Ashley, your allowance is more than my paycheck!

25 ASHLEY: Great. So let me give you some. It's not that big a

26   deal.

27 TINA: I appreciate it, but no. *(Pauses as if she's not sure she should*

28   *share this next part.)* See, I'm sponsoring this kid and I have

29   to send my check next week.

30 GILLY: Sponsoring a kid? For what? Some kind of camp?

31 TINA: No. Not a camp. It's so he can have food and clean water

32   and go to school and stuff.

33 KAREN: So who roped you into that?

34 ASHLEY: Someone guilt-tripped you and then reeled you in!

35 GILLY: What was it? Like one of those commercials that you flip

1   past 'cause they flash all those pictures of kids with their
2   ribs sticking out, trying to make you feel guilty?
3 KAREN: Yeah. They got you good.
4 TINA: It's not like that, you guys. I don't do this out of guilt. I
5   do it because I *want* to. It feels good knowing that I'm
6   making a difference. Even if it's only to one kid.
7 KAREN: Well, there you go! That's nothing when you think
8   about it. I mean in the whole scheme of things does one
9   kid even matter?
10 TINA: To Renaldo it matters. To him it's everything.
11 GILLY: Renaldo? Really? *(Obviously skeptical)*
12 TINA: Yeah, I even have a picture. *(Pulls a picture out of her purse*
13   *and shows it to the other girls. They aren't impressed.)*
14 ASHLEY: They probably mass-produce those pictures. Who
15   knows when they actually took this? He's probably a thirty-
16   year-old man by now.
17 KAREN: Ooooh. It's like on the Internet when you think you're
18   talking to some hot guy and it's probably some perv that
19   is old enough to be your grandfather.
20 GILLY: Ewwww. That's gross. That's why I always make them
21   send me a picture.
22 KAREN: *(Shaking head)* Gilly! It's the same thing! The perv can
23   send anybody's picture! Don't you get it?
24 ASHLEY: Remember last year when you kept messaging that
25   guy and the picture he sent was the same one we saw in
26   your mom's new picture frame? The guy had scanned a
27   fake picture!
28 KAREN: It happens all the time.
29 TINA: This isn't like that at all.
30 ASHLEY: Renaldo probably isn't even real. He's like a
31   Photoshop image or something.
32 TINA: *(Snatches picture back.)* Very funny. But we write to each
33   other and he's definitely a real kid.
34 KAREN: Anybody can write letters, Tina. You really can't know
35   for sure that you're not getting taken.

1   TINA: Sometimes you just have to have faith. I know Renaldo
2   is real and I know he needs me.
3   GILLY: *(Rolls eyes.)* OK. So you're saving this kid's life for exactly
4   how much?
5   TINA: Thirty-two dollars a month. *(The other girls look at each*
6   *other and then start laughing.)*
7   KAREN: Omigosh! You are so gullible!
8   GILLY: Yeah! You are so getting taken! Thirty-two dollars for ...
9   what was it? Food, water, school supplies, and more?
10   Thirty-two dollars won't even buy two skirts in this catalog!
11 ASHLEY: Who are you kidding? It won't buy one skirt in this
12   catalog!
13 TINA: I know! We're so spoiled! Don't you see? Spending that
14   kind of money when children are starving all around the
15   world.
16 ASHLEY: Whoa! Hold up with your little pity-party-bleeding-
17   heart-I'm-starving-to-death commercial.
18 KAREN: Yeah. You sound like my mother when she tells me to
19   eat everything on my plate because children are starving.
20   How is me eating everything going to help them anyway?
21 GILLY: For real. Let their governments take care of them. It's
22   not our fault they're letting their people starve.
23 ASHLEY: Really. It's not *our* responsibility.
24 TINA: I think it is. Everybody should try to give back something.
25 ASHLEY: Give back? We're teenagers for crying out loud! That's
26   what our parents are for!
27 GILLY: Yeah. I don't have any money to take care of the poor.
28 TINA: You just said that your dad gives you "ridiculous amounts
29   of money!"
30 GILLY: Not for things like that! For things I *need!*
31 TINA: Like the fifty-plus pairs of shoes you have? And the
32   matching purses?
33 GILLY: Well, I gotta look good.
34 TINA: *(Shaking head)* Some kids don't even have shoes, Gilly.
35 GILLY: That's not my fault, Tina. It's not like I'm stealing shoes

1   from the poor or anything.

2   ASHLEY: So we're just supposed to sit here and feel guilty for

3   everything we've got?

4   KAREN: Yeah. We're supposed to feel bad because we have

5   good homes and food to eat? We're supposed to sit here

6   and feel bad for all of that? Is that what you're saying?

7   TINA: No. We're not supposed to just sit here. *(Gets up.)* We're

8   supposed to *do* something. *(Exits.)*

9   KAREN: Well, I guess we'll be going to the mall without her!

Cheater

(3 Guys)
CHARACTERS:
>**John:** Friend of Kevin's who is concerned about cheating. Tries to convince Kevin that cheating is not the answer to his problems. Toward the end, he gets sucked into Kevin's way of thinking.
>
>**Kevin:** Has a lot of pressure to excel. Thinks cheating is his only option to guarantee good grades, scholarship, etc.
>
>**Adam:** Offers to help John study. Later tries to talk sense into John when he starts agreeing with Kevin about cheating.

SETTING:
>In a classroom right before class starts. Chairs should be three across with Kevin on far left and Adam on far right. For first part, Adam is into his homework and doesn't really pay attention to what is going on between Kevin and John.

1 *(KEVIN is writing answers on his hand and up his arm when JOHN*
2   *enters Stage Right and sits down beside KEVIN.)*
3 JOHN: *(In a loud stage whisper, like he's afraid they'll get caught.)*
4   Kevin! Mr. Reynolds will be here any minute. What are you
5   doing?
6 KEVIN: I'm putting a little insurance into getting an A, that's
7   what I'm doing.
8 JOHN: Are you crazy? That's cheating.
9 KEVIN: Sure can't get anything past you, can I? No wonder
10   you've got a big four-point-oh GPA.
11 JOHN: Very funny. But Mr. Reynolds has eyes like a hawk. You
12   know that! If he catches you, it's an automatic zero.
13 KEVIN: Exactly. *If* I get caught. That's why I won't get caught.
14 JOHN: Yeah, 'cause it won't be obvious at all when you're
15   reading up and down your arm.
16 KEVIN: That's why I sat in the back. And look, *(Pulls sleeve down*
17   *to cover arm)* I'll only sneak a peek when I need to.
18 JOHN: Why risk it?
19 KEVIN: Why? I'll tell you why. I've got three killer tests this
20   week, I'm scheduled to work almost every night, and I'm
21   borderline B in this class as it is.
22 JOHN: So? One B won't kill you.
23 KEVIN: Says the perfect student.
24 JOHN: Well, I might not have ever gotten one, but I'm pretty
25   sure they're harmless. You can always bring it up next
26   semester.
27 KEVIN: I can't. That'll be too late. College applications are due
28   now. It won't matter what I make after this.
29 JOHN: One B is not going to keep you out of college. Well,
30   maybe Harvard.
31 KEVIN: My dad says straight A's are the only way I'm ever going
32   to get a scholarship. Anywhere. Even a state school.
33   Otherwise, I can kiss the chance of college good-bye.
34 JOHN: Maybe he's just saying that now ... to get you to work
35   hard.

1   KEVIN: No. He means it. Apparently he spent what little he had
2   saved for my college on his motorcycle last year.
3   JOHN: The Harley?
4   KEVIN: That's the one. I guess his mid-life crisis was more
5   important than my future.
6   JOHN: Wow. That's rough. And a lot of pressure. *(Pause)* But is
7   cheating the way you really want to do it?
8   KEVIN: It's not that big a deal. Half the kids in these advanced
9   classes cheat — it's the only way to survive. I barely get
10   any sleep as it is.
11   JOHN: What if you get caught? What will your dad say then?
12   Don't you think he really cares more about your character
13   than a stupid A?
14   KEVIN: Yeah. You'd think so, wouldn't you? But all my dad cares
15   about is the end result. Heck, he'd *buy* me an A if he
16   could. *(Pauses and then laughs sarcastically.)* Well, maybe if
17   he hadn't blown all the money on the motorcycle that he
18   barely even rides. Honestly, I think he's scared of it.
19   JOHN: Maybe he'll sell it and give you the money for college.
20   KEVIN: Are you kidding? Apparently washing and waxing the
21   stupid thing is almost as cool as riding it.
22   JOHN: Come to think of it. I have seen him washing it a lot. But
23   I've never seen him ride it. You really think he's afraid of it?
24   That is so funny.
25   KEVIN: Yeah, it's a real laugh a minute. I'll be laughing all the
26   way *not* to college.
27   JOHN: Sorry. I didn't mean it that way.
28   KEVIN: I know. It's not your fault my dad doesn't care about my
29   future.
30   JOHN: Maybe he just wants you to earn it. I don't know what
31   my parents would do if I didn't have a scholarship in the
32   bag. I think they'd pay ... but who knows? Maybe they
33   wouldn't.
34   KEVIN: Yeah, right. The same parents that bought you a brand
35   new pickup for your sixteenth birthday would definitely *not*

1   pay your way to college.
2   JOHN: Well, you never know. *(Pause.)* And it wasn't brand new.
3   It was a demo, remember? It had like five thousand miles
4   on it or something.
5   KEVIN: Oh, poor thing. I forgot they got you that *used* piece of
6   crap. I think my car has ... hmmmm ... over a hundred-fifty
7   thousand miles on it. And it's missing two hubcaps, a
8   muffler, and the air conditioner hasn't worked since the
9   fifties. And don't forget the paint job! I've got more colors
10   on my car than your girlfriend has highlights in her hair!
11   JOHN: No need to get nasty, Kevin. I'm just trying to help.
12   KEVIN: Sorry. Guess I'm a little touchy. A life with no future can
13   do that to a person.
14   JOHN: You don't have to be so dramatic. I'm sure there are
15   other ways to get into college. You got any disabilities
16   you're hiding?
17   KEVIN: Does a freakishly long middle toe count?
18   JOHN: *(Laughing)* Probably not. What else have you got?
19   KEVIN: Think that's it.
20   JOHN: What about multi-cultural? Where are you from?
21   KEVIN: Uh, Indiana. Don't think I'll get anything for that.
22   JOHN: No, stupid. Your family. Your heritage. Where are they
23   from?
24   KEVIN: Uh ... Indiana. John, I am not multi-cultural. Look at
25   me. I'm as white as rice. I don't think you look at me and
26   think, hmmmm ... that guy's ethnic.
27   JOHN: There's got to be something else. *(Thinking)* You're poor,
28   aren't you? Maybe you can get a grant or something.
29   KEVIN: *I'm* poor. My parents aren't. Schools look at that. They
30   think just because your parents have money that they're
31   going to give it to you. They don't think they're going to
32   spend it on Harleys and Hawaiian vacations.
33   JOHN: Hawaii? When?
34   KEVIN: Right after graduation.
35   JOHN: They're taking you to Hawaii for graduation and you

1   didn't even tell me?
2   KEVIN: No. You're not listening, John. *They* are going to Hawaii.
3   Not me. Them. I think it's their "woo hoo we got the last
4   one out of the house" vacation.
5   JOHN: Oh, that's terrible. My parents would never go on
6   vacation without me.
7   KEVIN: Your parents don't go to the grocery without you, John.
8   They're going to freak when you're at college.
9   JOHN: I know. My mom is already crying.
10 KEVIN: My mom is crying because there's still six months left.
11 I think she has a secret calendar where she's counting
12 down the days until I leave.
13 JOHN: She does not! Your mom is going to be just as torn up
14 as mine. She just doesn't show it.
15 KEVIN: Yeah. That's what it is. Keep telling yourself that.
16 JOHN: Well, at least your parents don't suffocate you the way
17 mine do. It can be annoying, you know?
18 KEVIN: No. I don't know. But whatever. We all have our own
19 little dramas, don't we? Now stop whining about your
20 obviously "pitiful" *(Air quotes)* life so I can finish the
21 "dreaded cheating." *(Air quotes)*
22 ADAM: *(Finally stops studying and talks to them.)* Hey guys. I
23 heard you talking —
24 KEVIN: Great. What're you going to do, turn me in?
25 ADAM: No. Of course not. I just wanted to tell you that I'm
26 really good at chemistry. I'd be happy to help you study.
27 JOHN: See, Kevin. There is another way.
28 KEVIN: Maybe if you can cram a whole night of studying into
29 five minutes *(Glances at watch)* because that's about how
30 long we've got until Mr. Reynolds comes in.
31 ADAM: I'll do what I can ... *(Starts pulling out notes.)*
32 KEVIN: Who are you kidding? We all know five minutes of
33 cramming isn't going to help me.
34 ADAM: Well, we won't know until we try.
35 KEVIN: Thanks, but I think I'll stick with what I've got.

1 JOHN: You really think those scribbled notes on your hand and
2   up your arm are going to help? *(Inspecting arm)* You can
3   barely even read them.
4 KEVIN: It's a code. And they sure can't hurt. I think I know the
5   gist of things. I just need a little help. It's crazy that Mr.
6   Reynolds expects us to memorize all this anyway.
7 JOHN: It *is* a lot.
8 KEVIN: And when am I really going to need this? I mean, this is
9   a complete waste of brain cells. I think he just likes to
10   torture us.
11 JOHN: He does seem a lot happier on quiz days, doesn't he?
12 KEVIN: Of course he does! He loves seeing us suffer. Squirming
13   in our seats like pigs going to slaughter.
14 JOHN: For real! And have you noticed that whenever he writes
15   this stuff on the board he always has a book or notes in his
16   hands? He sure doesn't have this stuff memorized!
17 KEVIN: That's what I'm saying! Why should we? He's the
18   teacher. If anyone should know this baloney, it's him. What
19   a hypocrite, expecting us to know this by heart!
20 JOHN: Yeah! Pure hypocrisy!
21 KEVIN: That's why we should band together. Revolt against the
22   injustice. Come on, John! Cheat! Cheat! Cheat! *(JOHN,*
23   *caught in the moment, begins writing on his arm.)*
24 ADAM: *(ADAM grabs JOHN's arm to stop him.)* What are you
25   doing?
26 JOHN: You heard Kevin! We have to band together! Fight the
27   hypocrisy!
28 ADAM: This is ridiculous and you know it. Please tell me you're
29   not really buying into this load of bull.
30 JOHN: Well ... it does make sense.
31 KEVIN: That's right, John. Stay strong! Down with hypocrisy!
32   Up with cheating! Free the students! Free the students!
33 JOHN: *(Starts chanting as if in a trance.)* Free the students! Free
34   the students!
35 ADAM: *(ADAM grabs him by the shoulders and starts shaking him.)*

1   John! Listen to me! This is just Kevin's way of justifying
2   what he's doing. Don't let him suck you into this.
3 JOHN: *(Dazedly)* But the students ...
4 ADAM: The students are fine, John. Trust me. *(He pulls him out*
5   *of his chair.)* Come on, let's get you to the bathroom so you
6   can wipe that off your arm before Mr. Reynolds comes in
7   and sees it.
8 JOHN: *(Still in a daze, looks down at his arm, as if thinking "how*
9   *did that get there?")* ... my arm ... ?
10 ADAM: *(Leading JOHN off)* It's going to be alright ...
11 KEVIN: *(Calls after them.)* Free the students! Free the students!
12   Band together!

Shoplifter

(4 Girls)

CHARACTERS:

  Tracy: Shoplifts a bottle of nail polish.

  Alexis: Rough girl. Encourages Tracy; tells her shoplifting is no big deal.

  Kelly: Really upset that Tracy shoplifted. Tries to get her to return the polish.

  Gina: Tries to buy the polish for Tracy, but Tracy won't let her.

SETTING:

  Gina, Kelly, Tracy, and Alexis are walking in together from Stage Right. They stop Center Stage when Tracy takes a bottle of nail polish out of her purse.

1 TRACY: This is going to look so great with my new dress.
2 ALEXIS: That is a fabulous color!
3 KELLY: *(Looks behind her, then back at TRACY.)* Where did you get
4   that?
5 TRACY: The store, dummy. You know, the one we just left.
6 KELLY: But you didn't check out with anything.
7 TRACY: *(Waving fingers)* Five finger discount.
8 ALEXIS: Five finger discount! My favorite kind of sale!
9 GINA: Tracy! *(Grabbing at bottle)* You've got to take that back!
10 TRACY: *(Jerks the bottle out of GINA's reach.)* No way! It's perfect.
11   I've been looking everywhere for this shade!
12 ALEXIS: Ooooh. It's totally you!
13 KELLY: *(To TRACY)* Then buy it, don't steal it.
14 TRACY: Can't. I'm broke. I spent my last twenty dollars putting
15   gas in my car. And you know that's not going to last long.
16   I barely got half a tank for that!
17 KELLY: Then wait until you get paid again. You can buy it then.
18 TRACY: I have a date on Friday. I can't wait another week until
19   payday.
20 ALEXIS: And why should you? Don't listen to them. It's no big
21   deal. Everybody does it.
22 GINA: Look. Give it here. I'll buy it for you.
23 TRACY: Yeah, and what do you think's gonna happen when you
24   waltz back in with that and tell them I lifted it? They're
25   gonna call the cops, that's what.
26 ALEXIS: Yeah. You really don't want to do that. Trust me.
27 KELLY: *(Sarcastically to ALEXIS)* I'm sure you know everything
28   about cops, huh, Alexis?
29 ALEXIS: I know a few things.
30 KELLY: Big surprise there.
31 GINA: *(To TRACY)* They're not going to call the cops. I'm going
32   to take it back and pay for it.
33 TRACY: No way. You'd practically be turning me in. Besides,
34   you're making a big deal out of nothing.
35 KELLY: This isn't nothing.

1 TRACY: Oh, come on. Didn't you see the sign? Buy one get one
2   free.
3 KELLY: But you didn't buy one.
4 TRACY: *(Laughing)* I know. I just went ahead and got the free
5   one.
6 ALEXIS: Good one, Tracy! I'll have to use that sometime!
7 GINA: *(Ignoring ALEXIS — to TRACY)* That's not right and you
8   know it.
9 TRACY: Look. It's nothing. A stinking bottle of nail polish.
10   Everybody does it ... they practically expect it!
11 ALEXIS: That's right. They might as well put signs up that say
12   "Take me!"
13 TRACY: It's all part of the pricing, you know? The stores know
14   that people are going to shoplift little things like this, so
15   they up the price to make up for the loss.
16 KELLY: Well, maybe if people didn't actually steal then they
17   wouldn't have to do that.
18 TRACY: Yeah and maybe we shouldn't be letting kids starve all
19   over the world, Kelly.
20 GINA: What? Are you on drugs? You're comparing what you did
21   with world hunger? Are you kidding me?
22 TRACY: I'm just saying the world's not perfect. Things are what
23   they are.
24 KELLY: That is the most ridiculous thing I've ever heard. So you
25   think that just because the store can't afford to keep their
26   prices down because people are stealing from them that it
27   makes it OK to actually steal from them?
28 ALEXIS: It's a vicious cycle, isn't it?
29 TRACY: It is what it is. If they don't want people stealing, then
30   either lock things up better or lower the price. Simple as
31   that.
32 GINA: Simple as that? I've got a better one. How about, if you
33   don't like the prices, then don't shop there?
34 KELLY: Yeah, you're just justifying what you did with logic that
35   doesn't even make sense. If I use your logic then I could

1   get away with murder. I'd be like, hey, you shouldn't have
2   let me buy the gun if you didn't want me to kill people with
3   it. You're totally putting the responsibility of this on the
4   store! Like it's their fault you broke the law.
5 TRACY: Geez, Kelly. Calm your feathers. Nobody's committing
6   murder here.
7 GINA: *(Very sarcastically)* Oh, so that makes it OK.
8 ALEXIS: *(To TRACY)* Didn't know your friends were so uptight.
9   How do you stand it?
10 TRACY: Normally they're pretty cool.
11 KELLY: Guess maybe we lost our "coolness" when our best
12   friend became a thief right before our eyes.
13 GINA: Really, Tracy. I thought I knew you better than this. We've
14   been friends since kindergarten!
15 TRACY: So, nothing's changed. I'm still Tracy.
16 GINA: Not the Tracy I know. What's gotten in to you?
17 ALEXIS: What's it to you? You writing a book? *Life and Times of*
18   *Tracy McGuire?*
19 KELLY: Maybe you should stay out of this, Alexis.
20 GINA: In fact, maybe you should just stay out of Tracy's life.
21   Ever since you came along, it's been nothing but trouble.
22 ALEXIS: I think you're confusing the words "trouble" and
23   "exciting." Maybe Tracy's sick of hanging out with a bunch
24   of goody-two-shoes. *(Mocking)* Like, what do we want to do
25   tonight? Watch our hair grow, or, I know! We could pluck
26   our eyebrows! They're getting *so* bushy.
27 KELLY: *(Leaning into ALEXIS)* Actually, Alexis, I'd say you could
28   use a night with a pair of tweezers. You know that uni-
29   brows really never were in style. At least not on a girl. But
30   then again ... *(Looking her up and down as if to imply she's*
31   *not a girl anyway.)*
32 ALEXIS: Ooooh, Barbie here's getting mad. Watch out! She
33   might break a nail or something!
34 TRACY: Stop it! This is so stupid!
35 KELLY: She started it.

1 TRACY: Well, I'm ending it. This has gotten out of hand. No
2   harm was done. End of story, OK? *(Pleading)*
3 GINA: *(Silent for a second as if she wants to let it go but can't.)* What
4   if you'd gotten caught? What if they thought I was in on it?
5 TRACY: Oh, so that's it? Isn't it? The real problem. We sure
6   can't have anything tainting your saintly record, now can
7   we?
8 GINA: What are you talking about? Just because I don't steal
9   you think I'm some goody-two-shoes?
10 ALEXIS: That and about a million other reasons.
11 KELLY: Don't turn this around on her! Tracy, you're the one
12   who's wrong. Don't you feel the least bit guilty?
13 TRACY: *(Shrugging)* Nah. They can afford it. They charge way
14   too much anyway. I mean, come on. Over the years I've
15   paid for this a dozen times.
16 ALEXIS: That's right! They practically owe you for it!
17 KELLY: You haven't paid for it once, Tracy. That's the point.
18 TRACY: Don't get all righteous like you've never done anything
19   wrong. Maybe I should tell everyone about the time you
20   stole liquor out of your parents' stash.
21 KELLY: That hardly compares to this. I doubt my parents were
22   going to call the cops on me. We could've all gone to jail
23   because of you.
24 ALEXIS: *(Sarcastically)* Yeah, I hear that jail is overflowing with
25   dangerous shoplifters! They go real hard on them. Some
26   probably even get the electric chair!
27 GINA: *(Looks at ALEXIS with obvious disgust.)* Is everything a joke
28   to you?
29 ALEXIS: They would've called her parents. Talked rough to her.
30   Made her cry. Nobody was getting carted off to jail in
31   handcuffs.
32 GINA: Says the shoplifting expert.
33 ALEXIS: What can I say? I've been caught a few times. I'm not
34   as slick as my girl here. *(Puts her arm around TRACY.)*
35 GINA: Yeah, that's something to be proud of. "Meet Tracy, my

1   new best friend. She's got hands like lightning when it
2   comes to lifting things!"
3 ALEXIS: Lightning. I like it. Maybe that'll be her new nickname.
4 KELLY: Just shut up, Alexis. *(To TRACY)* Tracy, you might think
5   this is all a big game, but it's not. It's against the law.
6   Doesn't that mean anything to you?
7 TRACY: So is speeding but that sure doesn't stop you, does it?
8 KELLY: Now you're comparing this to speeding?
9 TRACY: The law is the law.
10 KELLY: Whatever. You've completely lost it. I'm outta here. *(She*
11   *walks off.)*
12 TRACY: It's a stupid bottle of polish. *(Yelling after KELLY)* It's not
13   like I held up a bank or something.
14 ALEXIS: *(Mockingly, acts like she has a gun.)* Put your hands in the
15   air and give me all your nail polish! *(She and TRACY laugh.)*
16 GINA: *(Ignores ALEXIS.)* Stealing is stealing, Tracy.
17 TRACY: *(Turns and gets in GINA's face.)* And annoying is annoying.
18 GINA: What's that supposed to mean?
19 ALEXIS: You sound worse than her mother.
20 TRACY: For real, Gina. Lighten up. You guys really blew this out
21   of proportion. Geez. It's a three-dollar bottle of polish.
22 GINA: Exactly. Was it really worth it? What will be next? CDs?
23   DVDs?
24 TRACY: Oh, come on. I'm not a thief.
25 GINA: You're not? Could've fooled me.
26 TRACY: For crying out loud. You are so dramatic. I take ...
27 GINA: Steal!
28 TRACY: OK. *Steal* one bottle of lousy polish and now I'm prison-
29   bound?
30 GINA: Well, you sure don't seem too guilt-ridden over it. You
31   know, everything starts somewhere.
32 TRACY: Yeah, well, everything has to *end* somewhere too. See
33   ya later, Gina. Oh, and here! *(Throws polish at her.)*
34   Something to remember me by! Come on, Alexis; let's get
35   out of here.

Revenge of the Rash

(3 Girls)

CHARACTERS:

　Emily: Popular, snotty teenage girl who attempts to prank Leah.

　Claire: Popular, snotty teenage girl whose mother keeps her supplied with bath and body accessories.

　Leah: Not-so-popular girl who is supposed to be the victim of Emily and Claire's locker room prank, only she catches on and turns the tables on them.

SETTING:

　Girls' locker room at school after P.E. class. Emily and Claire are there first, discussing the prank. When Leah enters, they try to convince her to take a shower so they can steal her clothes.

1   EMILY: This is going to be so great!
2   CLAIRE: I know! I wish we could see her face when she reaches
3   for her clothes and they're not there! She's going to freak!
4   EMILY: This will go down as the best prank in locker room
5   history!
6   CLAIRE: I wonder how long she'll stay in here? I mean, it's not
7   like she'll be able to go get help or anything! *(Giggling.)*
8   EMILY: Shhhh! Here she comes! *(LEAH enters the room.)*
9   EMILY and CLAIRE: Hey, Leah.
10 LEAH: *(Clearly surprised that they are talking to her. Even looks over*
11   *her shoulder to see if they're talking to someone else. Responds*
12   *timidly.)* Hey.
13 CLAIRE: Tough class, huh?
14 LEAH: Yeah ... pretty tough. *(Reaches into locker — can pretend to*
15   *do this — and takes out books or jacket.)*
16 EMILY: *(Looking LEAH up and down)* So, you're not going to
17   shower?
18 CLAIRE: Ewwww ... after a workout like that? Gross!
19 EMILY: Yeah, Mr. Gibson really made the class sweat today.
20 LEAH: Well, of course, I was going to ... *(Digging through bag,*
21   *stalling, because she really wasn't going to shower.)* I just
22   wasn't sure I had my shampoo, that's all. *(Keeps digging.)*
23   Darn. Looks like I left it at home.
24 EMILY: No prob. You can use mine. *(Digs in her bag and hands*
25   *her the bottle.)*
26 LEAH: Oh ... thanks ... *(Goes back to digging.)* ... Now if only I
27   could find my soap ...
28 CLAIRE: *(Digs in her bag.)* Try this. It's a great scent. Cherry
29   Blossom.
30 LEAH: *(Definitely suspicious of the girls being so nice to her.)* Oh ...
31   OK ... thanks. *(Takes it hesitantly.)*
32 CLAIRE: *(Very friendly)* No biggie. My mom sells this stuff, so
33   I've got tons of it at home.
34 EMILY: Last year for my birthday she gave me a whole basket of
35   samples.

1 CLAIRE: *(Snotty and offended)* **Well, it's not like that's** *all* **I got**
2   **you.**
3 EMILY: **I didn't say it was. Of course you got me something else.**
4   **I didn't mean to imply that you were cheap or anything.**
5   **Geez. Chill.**
6 CLAIRE: *(Sullen)* **You just made it sound like that's all I got —**
7 EMILY: *(To LEAH)* **So you're off to the shower then?**
8 LEAH: *(Still not sure why it means so much to them, so she's wary.)*
9   **Yeah, I guess. Let me just find —** *(Starts digging again.)*
10 EMILY: **Oh, for goodness sakes! What is it now?**
11 LEAH: **My towel?**
12 CLAIRE: **Here! Take mine!** *(Thrusts her towel at her.)*
13 LEAH: **But then what are you going to use?**
14 CLAIRE: **Me? I don't need a shower.**
15 LEAH: **But you just said Mr. Gibson really made us sweat.**
16 CLAIRE: **I believe I said "the class." He really made "the class"**
17   **sweat today. Me? I don't sweat.**
18 EMILY: **Nope. She doesn't. It's funny, too, because I don't either.**
19 LEAH: *(Leah is finally catching on that they're trying to get her into*
20   *the shower. She knows they're up to no good.)* **Really? Wow. I**
21   **sweat worse than a cat in a wool sweater.** *(Lifts arms.)* **I**
22   **mean look at these pits! I could be a football player!**
23 EMILY: *(Grimacing)* **Ewwww. That's so gross.**
24 LEAH: **I know. I've tried all kinds of deodorants but** *nothing*
25   **works. Not even the guy stuff.** *(Sniffs underarms.)* **Wow.**
26   **These babies really smell today!**
27 CLAIRE: **All the more reason for that shower ...** *(Trying to shoo*
28   *her off)*
29 LEAH: *(Stalling)* **One time I sweat through three layers of shirts!**
30   **Three layers! Can you believe that?** *(Pauses. Sits down on*
31   *bench.)* **I think there might be something wrong with my**
32   **sweat glands or something. I mean, seriously, this kind of**
33   **sweating just can't be normal, can it?**
34 EMILY: **Oh, I'm sure you're perfectly normal. Lots of people**
35   **sweat.**

1 CLAIRE: Yeah. Just not Emily or me.

2 LEAH: What if I have some sort of disease or something?
3 Instead of night sweats, I've got day sweats? That could be
4 pretty serious, couldn't it?

5 EMILY: I don't think one little symptom of sweating is anything
6 to get so worked up about.

7 LEAH: *(Chews lip and acts more scared.)* Sometimes I get this
8 rash ...

9 CLAIRE: *(Pulling back at her towel)* Did you say rash?

10 EMILY: *(Pulls towel back toward LEAH.)* Now, Claire. Stop being
11 paranoid. I'm sure it's nothing —

12 LEAH: Oh, it's *something* all right. I get these bumps and they
13 get all red and then they itch and —

14 CLAIRE: *(Clearly grossed out)* Maybe you should use Emily's
15 towel. I've got really sensitive skin.

16 LEAH: No. I couldn't. Don't worry I'll just take a shower when I
17 get home later.

18 EMILY and CLAIRE: No! *(LEAH acts taken aback by their strong*
19 *reaction. But now she knows for sure that they are up to*
20 *something.)*

21 EMILY: *(Much calmer)* What we meant was, it's no trouble. *(Digs*
22 *her towel out of her bag.)* Here. You can use mine. No
23 problem.

24 LEAH: *(Takes it slowly, watching EMILY's face.)* You're sure?
25 Because sometimes my rash oozes a little bit *(CLAIRE*
26 *makes a gagging face at this. EMILY is holding back her*
27 *disgust.)* and I'd hate to get that on your towel ...

28 EMILY: *(Really trying not to gag)* Really. It's no trouble at all.
29 Besides I've got plenty of towels at home. I'll just bring
30 another one tomorrow.

31 CLAIRE: So then, you're all set?

32 LEAH: *(Looking down at items in her arms)* Yeah. I guess ...
33 except ...

34 EMILY: *(Clearly forcing a smile)* Yes? Something else you need?

35 LEAH: I hate to ask.

1   **CLAIRE:** *(Under breath)* **Sure you do.**

2   **EMILY:** *(Shoving CLAIRE so she'll be quiet)* **What?** *(Digging through*

3   *CLAIRE's bag and pulling out items)* **Hair dryer? Hair spray?**

4   **Hair gel? You name it. Claire's got it all. Like a walking**

5   **beauty shop, actually.**

6   **LEAH:** *(Acts like she knows this is really a lot to ask but is loving*

7   *pushing them to the edge.)* **Well ... I could really use a loofah —**

8   **CLAIRE: A loofah?! You want to** *borrow* **a** *loofah?*

9   **EMILY:** *(Shoves her again with one hand while pulling a loofah out*

10   *of CLAIRE's bag with another.)* **Now, Claire. Stop making her**

11   **feel bad. The girl needs a loofah, and look! You've got a**

12   **loofah right here. Problem solved!** *(Hands the loofah to*

13   *LEAH, who acts very excited to get it.)*

14   **LEAH: That's really nice of you.**

15   **EMILY: What are friends for?** *(At this CLAIRE gives EMILY a look*

16   *that clearly says she's taking this too far.)*

17   **LEAH: Friends? Really? You think of me as a friend? I didn't**

18   **even think you knew my name.**

19   **EMILY: Of course we know your name ...** *(Obviously struggling to*

20   *remember it)*

21   **CLAIRE: Leah.**

22   **EMILY: Leah. How could we not know your name? We've had P.E.**

23   **with you all semester.**

24   **LEAH: Actually we've had P.E. together every year since third**

25   **grade.**

26   **EMILY: Really?** *(Gulps.)* **Third grade? Well, who would've thought ...**

27   **CLAIRE:** *(Trying to save her friend)* **I guess it's true that time**

28   **really flies, huh?**

29   **EMILY: Speaking of time flying ... you'd better hit that shower,**

30   **girl, or you're going to be late to class.**

31   **LEAH:** *(Glancing at watch)* **Gee. I don't know if I'm going to have**

32   **time —**

33   **CLAIRE: Sure you will. Take a speed shower. That's what I do**

34   **all the time.**

35   **EMILY: If you want, we'll stay here and keep track of the time**

1   for you. Make sure you don't take too long.
2   LEAH: Wow. You guys are being so nice. *(Tries another tactic to*
3   *avoid getting in the shower.)* Not at all like Grace said.
4   CLAIRE: *(Perks up.)* What? What did Grace say about us?
5   LEAH: Oh nothing. I shouldn't have said that. I hate gossip.
6   EMILY: *(Looks at CLAIRE and then at LEAH.)* Well, of course we do,
7   too. But if it's about us, we have a right to know! Don't we?
8   LEAH: I guess. I sure don't want to cause any trouble though.
9   CLAIRE: You won't cause any trouble. Maybe Grace misunderstood
10   something. Maybe this will give us a chance to clear it up.
11   See? Telling us is definitely the right thing to do!
12 LEAH: *(Looks around like she's afraid someone will overhear.)* Well,
13   she said that you girls are meaner than a bull at a rodeo!
14 EMILY: A bull at a rodeo? What a horrible thing to say!
15 CLAIRE: What a country backward thing to say! Was she
16   chewing on a blade of grass and spitting tobacco when she
17   said it? That doesn't even sound like something Grace
18   would say.
19 LEAH: *(Realizes what she's done and tries to cover.)* Yeah ... I know
20   ... I guess that just shows how upset she was ... it wasn't
21   like her *at all.*
22 EMILY: Well, did she say why? Why she thought we were like a
23   cow —
24 LEAH: Bull.
25 EMILY: Bull at a ... what was it? Rodeo? I don't even know what
26   that is!
27 LEAH: *(Excited)* Oh, it's where they have those riders who try to
28   stay on top of those wild bulls; all the while those bulls are
29   bucking up a storm and acting crazy!
30 CLAIRE: *(Narrows her eyes at LEAH.)* You seem to know an awful
31   lot about rodeos.
32 LEAH: *(Looks down quickly to avoid her eyes.)* Just what I've seen
33   on TV. I've never really been to one ...
34 EMILY: *(Still focused on what GRACE said.)* So did she say why?
35 LEAH: *(Happy to feed the fire and take the focus off herself)*

1   Something about backstabbing and a boy named —
2   CLAIRE: Jacob? Is she still spouting off about that?
3   LEAH: *(Relieved that they supplied the name.)* **Yeah. Jacob. I think**
4   **that was it!**
5   CLAIRE: Well, she can just get over it. He liked *me*, not *her*. And
6   Emily just delivered the note. Grace has some nerve
7   talking bad about her!
8   EMILY: Really! I didn't do anything.
9   LEAH: I knew I shouldn't have told you. Now you're both upset.
10 CLAIRE: Of course we're upset! Grace is a little two-faced liar.
11   Acting like I took Jacob from her.
12 EMILY: This just burns me up!
13 CLAIRE: I know! Look at me! I'm breaking out in a sweat! *(Pulls*
14   *towel back from LEAH and starts dabbing her face.)*
15 EMILY: Me, too! *(Wipes face with towel.)* **And we never sweat!**
16   *(LEAH lets them do this for a second, watching them wipe the*
17   *towel all over their faces.)*
18 LEAH: Um ... Emily ... Claire ...
19 EMILY and CLAIRE: What?
20 LEAH: Remember that rash I was telling you about? *(EMILY and*
21   *CLAIRE stop wiping their faces with the towel and look at*
22   *LEAH, shocked. They know what's coming.)* **Well, I have some**
23   **on my arm ... and I think it might have gotten on your towel**
24   ... *(EMILY and CLAIRE rush to other side of stage and*
25   *pantomime turning on the shower, stripping off clothes, and*
26   *getting in — frantically. LEAH gathers their clothes and all the*
27   *bags and walks Offstage.)*

8th Grade Bash

(2 Girls, 2 Guys, 2 Either)
CHARACTERS:

Heather: Girl who loves to shop. More into the social aspect of school than studying.

Lesley: Girl who wants to leave middle school with a bang.

Justin: Guy who is kind of a goof. Doesn't make good grades. They're afraid to trust him with any real responsibility.

Casey: Guy who helps make games for the carnival. Real go-getter.

Student 1: 6th grader who wants to help.

Student 2: Another 6th grader who wants to help.

SETTING:

Middle school, at lunch. Group is sitting around talking.

1   HEATHER: These next few months are going to go by so fast.
2   CASEY: I know. I can't believe we're getting ready to graduate
3   from middle school.
4   LESLEY: Where did the years go?
5   JUSTIN: Seemed like they took forever to me.
6   HEATHER: Well, for you they did. How many times did you take
7   Pre-Algebra?
8   JUSTIN: Can I help it that Mrs. Fink doesn't know how to
9   teach?
10 LESLEY: Hey, didn't you have Mrs. Fink, Casey?
11 CASEY: Yup.
12 LESLEY: So what'd you make?
13 CASEY: All A's.
14 HEATHER: Genius. *(All laugh, nudge JUSTIN.)*
15 JUSTIN: Anyway. I can't believe this is it. Ten weeks, three
16   days, and six hours, and then we'll officially be high
17   schoolers!
18 CASEY: Yeah, just a few months from now we'll be back in
19   school!
20 HEATHER: Don't remind me!
21 LESLEY: At least we'll be treated like adults. Make our own
22   decisions.
23 JUSTIN: I hear that they don't even take attendance in high
24   school. Like, you can skip whenever you want.
25 CASEY: That is so not true! My sister gets in huge trouble for
26   skipping all the time!
27 JUSTIN: Well, it's got to be better than the way we get treated
28   around here.
29 HEATHER: Yeah, I can't believe how they still make us walk in
30   single file lines around here. It's so kindergarten.
31 CASEY: Don't worry about that at the high school. My sister
32   said one girl got trampled so bad during change of class
33   that she had to be hospitalized!
34 JUSTIN: Cool.
35 LESLEY: That is so *not* cool. I don't want to get killed my first

1   year in high school!
2 HEATHER: Really! There's so much to look forward to —
3   driving, Prom, basketball games — it's going to be
4   awesome.
5 LESLEY: *(Pause.)* It will be a little sad leaving middle school
6   behind.
7 CASEY: I'm going to hate being the low man on the totem pole
8   again. Being a freshman is going to stink.
9 HEATHER: And I'm going to miss seeing you guys every day.
10   Who knows if we'll even have any classes together!
11 LESLEY: My luck, I'll get stuck in a class where I won't know
12   anyone!
13 CASEY: *(Pulls out cell phone.)* Hey! That's what text messaging
14   is for! We won't lose touch.
15 JUSTIN: Here's to cell phones! *(Pause as everyone raises their cell*
16   *phones up in a cheer.)*
17 LESLEY: I was just thinking. Do you think we made a difference
18   here? You know, left our mark?
19 JUSTIN: I know I did! Have you guys seen the locker room
20   where I spray painted my name? I had to come three
21   Saturdays for that one!
22 CASEY: You could've just left your gym shoes behind! *(Waves*
23   *hand in front of nose.)* That sure would've left a mark!
24 HEATHER: They put one of my sculptures from Advanced Art in
25   the display case up front.
26 CASEY: The football team won state finals! Woo hoo!
27 JUSTIN: Yeah, too bad all you did was warm the bench!
28 CASEY: Well, I was still on the team!
29 HEATHER: Only 'cause the team needed a tutor!
30 LESLEY: That's all great. But do you think we made a real
31   difference?
32 JUSTIN: Well, I made a difference to most of the girls in the
33   eighth grade class!
34 HEATHER: Funny! And so untrue! Unless getting turned down
35   by half the girls in class is what you call a difference!

1 JUSTIN: Better than getting turned down by all!

2 LESLEY: *(Trying to get everyone back on track)* **Well, anyway,**

3   that's why I've been thinking about this thing. How we

4   need to do something big. You know, go out with a bang

5   somehow. Really make a difference.

6 CASEY: Like what?

7 LESLEY: I don't know. Something to get everyone's attention.

8   Like a play, or a show ...

9 HEATHER: How about a talent show? You know how I love to

10   sing. *(Starts belting it out — badly.)* **"Somewhere over the**

11   rainbow ... "

12 JUSTIN: *(Fingers in ears)* **Make it stop! Please, make it stop!**

13 CASEY: That's great, Heather. We'll get everyone running for

14   that! Running *away*, that is!

15 HEATHER: Jealous.

16 LESLEY: I know! How about a carnival — an old-fashioned

17   carnival — and the eighth graders can do all the work!

18 HEATHER: *(Still pouting)* **Yeah, 'cause that would be much**

19   better.

20 LESLEY: We could have a puppet show!

21 CASEY: And one of those dart throwing booths!

22 JUSTIN: Yeah, we can make Mrs. Fink the target!

23 HEATHER: *(Perking back up)* **How about a kissing booth?**

24 ALL: Heather!

25 HEATHER: Just saying ... you've got to have something to

26   attract people.

27 JUSTIN: Free popcorn?

28 CASEY: Free popcorn? I don't think that's enough to bring in a

29   crowd.

30 LESLEY: Everything should be free! We'll get stores to donate

31   stuff!

32 HEATHER: *(Perking back up)* **Ooooh, ooooh! I could do that! You**

33   know I love going to the mall!

34 LESLEY: We'll have giveaways and prize booths! And game

35   booths where you throw stuff and —

1 JUSTIN: Slow down, Lesley! I think you've had a little too much
2   caffeine!
3 LESLEY: Really! You're making my head spin! Why don't we all
4   jot some ideas down and we'll get together tomorrow after
5   school and talk about it! *(ALL exit. STUDENT 1 walks across*
6   *stage with a sign reading "TOMORROW". The group walks back*
7   *On-stage. HEATHER is carrying several bags.)*
8 CASEY: Wow! Did you get your allowance today, Heather? I
9   thought you were getting donations! Not shopping!
10 JUSTIN: How many pairs of shoes are you up to now? One-fifty-
11   three?
12 HEATHER: Funny, guys. I just picked up a few things to start
13   on the puppets.
14 CASEY: Puppets?
15 HEATHER: Yeah. For the carnival, remember? Lesley and I got
16   some ideas from the library.
17 LESLEY: They're going to be so cool. We're making them out of
18   old socks.
19 JUSTIN: *(Leans down and acts like he's going to take his shoes off.)*
20   Here, I've got a pair you can have.
21 HEATHER: *(Shoves him.)* No thanks! We don't want to kill
22   people!
23 LESLEY: So did you guys come up with some ideas?
24 CASEY: *(Pulls a piece of paper out of his pocket and shows it to the*
25   *group.)* I've designed a dartboard and a prize wheel. *(They*
26   *all "ooooh" and "ahhhh" over it.)*
27 LESLEY: What about you, Justin?
28 JUSTIN: My dog ate it?
29 LESLEY: *(Shakes head, smiling.)* That's OK, Heather and I have
30   come up with plenty of ideas. *(Pulls out more papers.)*
31 HEATHER: So do you think we could pull this off by next
32   Saturday? I know it's fast, but I think we could do it. I
33   checked with Mr. Sullivan and he was on board. Said he
34   loved seeing his students take such initiative!
35 LESLEY: Wow. We'll have to work fast! Casey, you can work on

1   the dartboard and prize wheel, Heather and I will work on

2   the puppets and prizes ... and Justin ...

3 JUSTIN: What? What can I do?

4 HEATHER: Uh ... *(Clearly not sure what JUSTIN can contribute.)*

5 CASEY: *(Gets an idea.)* How about PR?

6 JUSTIN: PR?

7 LESLEY: Yeah! You'd be perfect!

8 JUSTIN: *(Stands up and salutes.)* PR man at your service!

9   *(Everyone laughs as two 6TH GRADERS enter.)*

10 STUDENT 1: Hey, we overheard what you were talking about

11   and we'd like to help.

12 STUDENT 2: Yeah, it sounds cool. What can we do?

13 STUDENT 1: I like to bake. I can coordinate a bake sale or

14   cakewalk or something.

15 HEATHER: *(They clearly look down their noses at the 6TH*

16   *GRADERS.)* We weren't planning on having a bake sale.

17 CASEY: Or a cakewalk.

18 STUDENT 2: Oh. Well, I'm sure I could come up with something

19   else.

20 HEATHER: *(Looks them up and down.)* Actually, there isn't much

21   left to do.

22 STUDENT 1: We can paint.

23 STUDENT 2: Or help with decorations.

24 JUSTIN: I think we've got it all covered. But ... uh ... thanks

25   anyway. *(6TH GRADERS walk off, shaking heads, shrugging*

26   *shoulders.)*

27 HEATHER: Can you believe that? Sixth graders wanting to help!

28 CASEY: Really. Like we'd be caught dead hanging with them.

29 JUSTIN: I thought the bake sale sounded great!

30 HEATHER: Of course! Anything to do with food!

31 LESLEY: It would've been nice to have some help. And they

32   seemed really nice.

33 HEATHER: Oh, Lesley. You're always so softhearted. One of

34   these days you've got to realize the point of being an eighth

35   grader! We're at the top of the food chain! We're supposed

1   to eat those kids for lunch!

2 CASEY: Yeah! Our number one job is to look down on everyone

3   else!

4 HEATHER: Besides, they get to come. What more do they want?

5   We do all the work and they can have all the fun!

6 LESLEY: *(Standing up)* Speaking of work, we'd better get

7   started. Let's check back in next Friday, OK? Same time,

8   same place?

9 ALL: Sounds good. *(ALL exit. STUDENT 2 walks across stage with*

10   *a sign reading "FRIDAY." The group walks back On-stage.)*

11 LESLEY: I am so tired!

12 CASEY: Between midterms and getting ready for the carnival, I

13   don't think I've slept all week!

14 HEATHER: I know! Lesley has been working me to death! I think

15   I've been painting game booths in my sleep!

16 JUSTIN: I can't believe it got here so fast ... wasn't it just last

17   week, like, a second ago?

18 LESLEY: Really. This whole thing has been a blur! But it is so

19   going to be worth it! They'll be talking about the eighth

20   grade carnival for years!

21 HEATHER: That's right, guys! This is our chance! Our big

22   chance to make a difference!

23 CASEY: I can't wait to see what people think about the

24   dartboard!

25 LESLEY: And the sock puppets!

26 JUSTIN: And don't forget the popcorn! I had to practically give

27   my left arm to borrow that machine!

28 LESLEY: It's going to be so great. Just twenty-four hours 'til the

29   carnival of the century! *(ALL exit. STUDENT 1 walks across*

30   *stage with a sign reading "MONDAY." The group enters, clearly*

31   *bummed and upset.)*

32 LESLEY: I just don't get it. We worked so hard ...

33 CASEY: I came to school on a Saturday ... and for what?

34   Nobody even came.

35 HEATHER: Really. Not even those sixth graders who wanted to

1   help so badly.

2 LESLEY: I just don't get it. Everything was free. It's not like it
3   would've cost them anything.

4 JUSTIN: *(Eating a handful of popcorn)* I thought at least the smell
5   would bring 'em in.

6 HEATHER: It just doesn't make any sense. I don't even know
7   why we bothered.

8 CASEY: Really, Lesley. "Make a difference." "Go out with a
9   bang." "Do something big." Well, we did something big all
10   right. A big waste of our time and money! *(All grumble.)*

11 LESLEY: Well, excuse me for caring. For wanting to be
12   remembered. For wanting to throw the carnival of the
13   century! I can't help it that no one came!

14 HEATHER: Maybe we needed more signs.

15 CASEY: Yeah ... come to think of it ... I don't remember seeing
16   any signs ... *(Everyone turns to look at JUSTIN.)* You *did* put
17   up the signs, didn't you?

18 JUSTIN: Why is everyone looking at me?

19 LESLEY: Justin! You were in charge of the signs!

20 JUSTIN: Who says? I don't remember anything about that!

21 HEATHER: *(Stands up and salutes.)* PR Man at your service!

22 JUSTIN: Dudes! That's what PR means? Signs and posters?

23 LESLEY: Duh! What'd you think?

24 JUSTIN: I wasn't sure but I thought it had something to do with
25   preaching and reaching. I even wrote this speech ... *(Pulls*
26   *crumpled paper out of pocket.)* How do you get signs and
27   posters out of PR?

28 CASEY: Public relations!

29 HEATHER: You gotta be kidding me. You mean to tell me there
30   wasn't even *one* sign?

31 JUSTIN: Well, at least you guys told people about it, right?

32   *(Everyone looks at each other, shrugging.)*

33 HEATHER: I was too busy painting ...

34 LESLEY: ... and making puppets.

35 CASEY: And making dartboards!

1   JUSTIN: So you guys didn't tell anyone? Didn't talk it up in
2   class? Didn't spread the word?
3   LESLEY: *(To JUSTIN)* What about you?
4   JUSTIN: I was too busy writing my speech. *(Everybody groans.)*
5   CASEY: I can't believe all this hard work was for nothing!
6   LESLEY: *(Jumps up.)* Maybe not — remember, one day we'll be
7   *seniors!* *(They all groan and exit, leaving LESLEY On-stage by*
8   *herself.)*
9   LESLEY: Hey, guys! Wait up! Come on! Don't be like this ... It'll
10   be great!

K-I-S-S-I-N-G

(2 Girls)
CHARACTERS:
   Mattie: Middle-school-aged sister with lots of questions about boys.
   Mary: High-school-aged sister, more sophisticated, seems to have all the answers when it comes to boys.

SETTING:
   The two sisters are camping out. At first, they're spying on their parents who are outside by the fire. Then they get caught up in their own conversation about kissing.

1 MATTIE: Mary. *(Nudges MARY.)* You awake?
2 MARY: *(Sits up on elbows.)* Yeah, I can't believe we're supposed
3   to sleep on the ground. When Mom and Dad said "a
4   weekend away," I thought they meant in a hotel. Tent
5   camping stinks.
6 MATTIE: Really. I can feel every little pebble poking my back.
7 MARY: Like "The Princess and the Pea"? I guess that makes
8   Mom the wicked queen. Wait until I tell her ... Mom ...
9 MATTIE: *(Puts her hand over MARY's mouth.)* Shhhh! They'll hear
10   you. And they don't want to be disturbed. Remember?
11 MARY: I remember. Why else would I be stuck in a tent with you
12   when it's only ten o'clock? At home I wouldn't be in bed for
13   another three hours!
14 MATTIE: *(Points out toward "parents.")* What do you suppose
15   they're talking about?
16 MARY: Who knows? Mom said the counselor told them they
17   need to spend some quality time together. To "reconnect."
18   I don't know why they had to come here to do that.
19   Couldn't they "reconnect" at home?
20 MATTIE: Really. Better yet. They could've come camping
21   *without* us.
22 MARY: I know. I'm perfectly capable of baby-sitting you for a
23   weekend. Only Mom thinks I'd throw a wild party or
24   something.
25 MATTIE: Well, you did throw a party the last time they left us
26   alone for the night.
27 MARY: Don't remind me. I'll be paying for that mistake for the
28   rest of my life. I think Mom yelled at me for three days
29   straight.
30 MATTIE: *(Looking back out at parents.)* At least they're not
31   fighting.
32 MARY: Oh, no. They've been nice and lovey with each other all
33   day. Like they're on a second honeymoon or something.
34   Pretty soon, they'll be kissing and hugging like a couple of
35   teenagers.

1   MATTIE: Oh, gross! Why would they want to do that?
2   MARY: 'Cause when you love someone, that's what you do.
3   MATTIE: I know that. But not parents! They're not supposed to
4   make out. Especially not with us around.
5   MARY: Sorry, chicklet. Fact of life. Besides, why do you think
6   they made us go to bed so early?
7   MATTIE: It's not like they were paying any attention to us
8   anyway.
9   MARY: I guess it's better to see them kissing all the time than
10   fighting.
11 MATTIE: I don't know ... I think I still prefer the fighting.
12   (Scrunches face in disgust.) Have you ever kissed a boy
13   before?
14 MARY: Kind of. Last year, Chris Morton gave me a kiss and I
15   kissed him back but it wasn't a real kiss.
16 MATTIE: What do you mean a real kiss? Did you really kiss him
17   or not?
18 MARY: There's a difference in how you kiss Mom and Dad and
19   how you kiss someone you love, and even then, it's not
20   always a real kiss.
21 MATTIE: Duh. I am in middle school. I know the difference
22   between kissing a relative and kissing a boy. But how do
23   you "not really" kiss a boy?
24 MARY: No chemistry.
25 MATTIE: You've got to have chemistry for it to count?
26 MARY: Yeah. Your lips should tingle and you should get all light-
27   headed and stuff. Otherwise — like kissing a relative.
28 MATTIE: Huh. There's this girl in eighth grade that missed her
29   bus because this boy kissed her and then she forgot her
30   bus number. Her mom had to come get her. Do you think
31   that was a real kiss?
32 MARY: I'd say a kiss that makes you forget your bus number is
33   definitely a real kiss.
34 MATTIE: Even though it was only on her cheek?
35 MARY: (Laughs.) That guy must pack a powerful kiss — if he

1   only had to kiss her on the cheek to give her temporary
2   amnesia.
3 MATTIE: So you didn't forget anything after you kissed Chris?
4 MARY: Nope. Not a thing. Though I would've liked to have
5   forgotten that I actually kissed him.
6 MATTIE: And your lips didn't tingle even a little bit?
7 MARY: Nope. It was like kissing our brother ... if we had one.
8   *(Looks out at parents.)* Let's hope the counselor didn't
9   suggest *that* as part of therapy. The last thing we need is
10   a brother ... or sister.
11 MATTIE: Really.
12 MARY: *(Nudges MATTIE.)* It's bad enough having one pesky little
13   sister.
14 MATTIE: Funny. If I wasn't here, who would you boss around?
15 MARY: Good point.
16 MATTIE: *(Girls are quiet for a minute.)* Would you teach me how to
17   kiss?
18 MARY: Gross!
19 MATTIE: I don't mean kiss me, just tell me how.
20 MARY: Why? You got a boy in mind?
21 MATTIE: Not really. But I am getting older. It's going to happen
22   some day, you know.
23 MARY: Not if you keep eating those nasty onion rings! No boy
24   will come within ten feet of you.
25 MATTIE: I know. That's my boy repellent — for now. When I stop
26   eating them — watch out! Boys will be running to come
27   kiss me!
28 MARY: Yeah, I'm sure they'll be knocking each other over just
29   to get a kiss from you.
30 MATTIE: Could happen. So what do I do? I need to be prepared,
31   right?
32 MARY: Well, first you want to make sure that you *do* have
33   breath that won't kill a dog. So, if you think you're going
34   to be in a situation where it could actually happen — you
35   know, in about ten million years or so —

1 MATTIE: You're so funny — for a girl who probably doesn't even
2   know how to kiss —
3 MARY: Oh, I know how! Believe me!
4 MATTIE: So you say.
5 MARY: Look, do you want my help or not?
6 MATTIE: OK. So fresh breath. I get it. I'll be sure to carry a
7   whole purse full of breath mints.
8 MARY: That's a start. The next step is to make sure you look
9   kissable.
10 MATTIE: Look kissable? How do you look kissable?
11 MARY: Well, you don't want boogers in your nose ...
12 MATTIE: Duh.
13 MARY: Or gross chapped lips. You know how you sometimes
14   have those little pieces of skin hanging off your lips ... well,
15   you definitely don't want any of those.
16 MATTIE: Got it. Use lots of lip balm.
17 MARY: The next step is to let the boy know you want to kiss
18   him.
19 MATTIE: Like in a note?
20 MARY: Omigosh. No. Not in a note. With your body language.
21 MATTIE: How do I do that?
22 MARY: You don't move away if he starts standing real close to
23   you.
24 MATTIE: Mrs. Arrowwood calls that our "personal space." She
25   gets real mad if she sees us getting too close to each
26   other. But that's because she's afraid of lice. One year her
27   whole class got them! She was so paranoid about getting
28   them that she cut her hair so short she looked like a man!
29   Too bad for her that she got them anyway! Ever since, she
30   has *strict* rules about personal space.
31 MARY: Well, then you won't want to be kissing in her room.
32 MATTIE: Oh no! I would never! She'd suspend me for weeks! So
33   what's the next step?
34 MARY: We're still on the last one. You can't just let him in your
35   personal space to give him a clue that you want to kiss

1   him. Boys are dense. It takes a whole lot more than that.
2   MATTIE: Like what? A sign? Poster? Billboard? Flashing neon
3   lights?
4   MARY: Just about. You have to be flirty. You know, twist your
5   hair around your finger, laugh at everything he says — but
6   not too loud or you'll scare him off ...
7   MATTIE: This all sounds pretty complicated.
8   MARY: It is. You don't want to mess up and be known as the
9   worst kisser in school.
10 MATTIE: I can definitely say that I don't want to be known for
11   that. So what else?
12 MARY: When he moves in for the kiss, you'll need to be ready.
13   You have to move just right or you'll bump heads.
14 MATTIE: That would be bad.
15 MARY: Real bad. And you have to make sure he's actually coming
16   in to kiss you and not just leaning in to tell you something
17   or you'll look like an idiot if you start puckering up!
18 MATTIE: OK, so no puckering until I'm absolutely sure.
19 MARY: Once his lips are on yours, you'll need to exert the right
20   amount of pressure.
21 MATTIE: Right amount of pressure? Are we talking about lips or
22   tires here?
23 MARY: Believe me, you do *not* want to be to loose and fishy, and
24   you definitely do not want to be too hard. You have to be
25   soft but not too soft. Firm but not too firm.
26 MATTIE: *(Giggling)* Sounds like kissing for Goldilocks.
27   Everything has to be "just right."
28 MARY: Pretty much.
29 MATTIE: So how will I know what's "just right"?
30 MARY: Practice. I saw a movie once where a girl practiced
31   kissing on her arm. You could do that. You'll be able to tell
32   if you pressing too hard or too soft.
33 MATTIE: OK. *(Kisses arm very quickly.)*
34 MARY: You have to do it longer than that. A real kiss takes
35   time.

1 MATTIE: OK, OK. *(Kisses arm again, slower.)*
2 MARY: Good. Now, close your eyes.
3 MATTIE: Why? What are you going to do to me?
4 MARY: I'm not going to do anything.
5 MATTIE: Promise?
6 MARY: I promise.
7 MATTIE: Pinkie swear?
8 MARY: Fine. Pinkie swear. *(They hook pinkies.)* **Now try it again**
9   **and close your eyes. You can't stare the boy down. It'll**
10   **make him nervous. Besides, it's more romantic if your eyes**
11   **are shut.**
12 MATTIE: But if we both close our eyes, how are we going to find
13   each other's lips?
14 MARY: *(Sighing)* **You have to time it just right. As he's moving**
15   **in for the kiss, you keep your eyes open. When your lips**
16   **meet, you close your eyes.**
17 MATTIE: Got it. *(Closes eyes and starts toward her arm. Stops and*
18   *opens her eyes again.)* **But when do you open them again?**
19 MARY: *(Sarcastically)* **After you've graduated high school.**
20   *(Nudges her.)* **When the kiss is over, dummy. You don't want**
21   **to stand there with your eyes closed forever. He'll think**
22   **he's put you in a coma or something.**
23 MATTIE: The second it's over, or wait a minute?
24 MARY: As soon as he moves away, you open your eyes.
25 MATTIE: What about peeking? Should I peek to see what's
26   going on?
27 MARY: No! You definitely do not peek. He'll think you're bored
28   or something.
29 MATTIE: How would he know unless he's peeking, too?
30 MARY: Just don't peek, OK?
31 MATTIE: Fine. So that's it? Everything I need to know about
32   kissing?
33 MARY: Pretty much.
34 MATTIE: OK. I think I've got it: Fresh breath, look kissable, let
35   him in my personal space, use the right amount of

1   pressure, and close my eyes.

2 MARY: You're all set. For now. But you might want to go ahead

3   and get that first kiss over with before next week ...

4 MATTIE: Before next week? Why?

5 MARY: You get your braces then, right?

6 MATTIE: Yeah. What does that have to do with kissing?

7 MARY: *(Dramatically)* Having braces changes everything!

8 MATTIE: *(Obviously panicked)* It does? Oh no! Why? What do I

9   need to know?

10 MARY: *(Shaking her head and smiling)* Just practice your arm

11   kissing, OK, Mattie?

Dance Fever

(2 Girls, 2 Guys)
CHARACTERS:

Paige: Confident girl who thinks she knows everything about guys.

Misty: Shy girl who is completely clueless when it comes to guys. She believes everything Paige tells her about the ins and outs of getting a boy to dance.

Stephen: Guy who thinks he knows everything about girls.

Cory: Very nervous guy who is terrified of dancing with a girl. Takes advice from his friend Stephen who convinces him that he knows everything about girls.

SETTING:

School dance. The two girls stand on one side of the stage having one conversation, while the two guys stand on the other side having their own conversation. The skit will alternate sides: while one side is talking, the other side freezes, and vice versa.

1 PAIGE: You just have to go ask him.

2 MISTY: It's not that easy, Paige. You don't just walk up to a guy

3   and say —

4 CORY: "Do you wanna dance?" Really? You think it's that easy?

5   She'll take one look at me and walk off.

6 STEPHEN: Why? What's wrong with you? You look fine to me.

7 CORY: I look like a guy who doesn't have a clue about how to

8   dance with a girl.

9 STEPHEN: Well, you don't. But she doesn't know that.

10 CORY: I think I'd like to keep it that way.

11 STEPHEN: Come on. Don't chicken out now. Just let —

12 PAIGE: — him take the lead. That way he'll never know that it's

13   your first time dancing with a boy.

14 MISTY: But it *is* my first time dancing with a boy.

15 PAIGE: Yeah, well you don't want him knowing that. You have

16   to appear confident —

17 STEPHEN: — but not too confident. You don't want her to think

18   you're a jerk or anything.

19 PAIGE: Try to avoid his eyes. It'll make you more mysterious.

20 STEPHEN: You've got to look straight into her eyes when you

21   ask her. Shows you care and that she can trust you.

22 CORY: Trust me? I don't want to marry the girl. Just dance with

23   her.

24 STEPHEN: Believe me. To a girl, it's a whole lot more than just

25   a dance.

26 CORY: What do I say to her then? You know, when we are

27   actually dancing. Am I supposed to start planning our

28   wedding, or what?

29 STEPHEN: *(Laughing)* No. It's better if you don't say anything.

30   Let her do all the talking.

31 PAIGE: Boys love to do all the talking! So don't say much while

32   you're dancing. Give him time to talk about himself. Guys

33   love that.

34 STEPHEN: Girls like it when they feel like they're in charge. So

35   you just have to let her take the lead. That way she'll never

1   know that you really can't dance either.

2   CORY: I'm pretty sure when I step on her feet she'll figure that
3   one out real quick.

4   STEPHEN: Just keep a lot of distance between you. Keep your
5   arms stiff and hold her away from you as much as
6   possible. She'll like that because it shows that you respect
7   her.

8   CORY: Like this? *(Holds arms out stiff — like Frankenstein.)*

9   STEPHEN: Not that stiff! You don't want to look like a guy who
10   should have bolts sticking out of his neck. *(Pushes at*
11   *CORY's arms, near the elbows.)* **Loosen these up a little bit**
12   **and then —**

13   PAIGE: — make sure that you get close enough to be able to
14   put your head on his shoulder. Guys like it when you do
15   that during the slow dances.

16   MISTY: Head on his shoulder? Look at him! I'd have to stand on
17   my tiptoes to reach his shoulder.

18   PAIGE: Well, get as close as you can. If he doesn't hold you
19   close, that's a warning sign.

20   MISTY: A warning sign? Of what?

21   PAIGE: I don't know. That he's not really in to you. Or maybe
22   B.O.

23   MISTY: B.O.? I do *not* have B.O.

24   PAIGE: Not yet. But wait until you get nervous and start
25   sweating. Make sure —

26   STEPHEN: — that you wear *lots* of deodorant and *lots* of
27   cologne. Here, use some of mine. *(Hands CORY a spray*
28   *bottle.)* **Don't be skimpy on it. You don't want her gagging**
29   **when you take her in your arms.**

30   CORY: *(Coughing from the spray)* It's a little strong, isn't it? I
31   think she'll be able to smell me from over here.

32   STEPHEN: Don't worry. It wears off fast. Maybe you should go.

33   CORY: I can't go over there now! She'd need a gas mask to get
34   near me!

35   STEPHEN: I think you smell great!

1   CORY: You would! But that's probably because you singed out
2   your nose hairs with that flaming marshmallow last year at
3   camp.
4   STEPHEN: *(Rubs nose, like he's remembering.)* Can I help it if the
5   stupid thing went up like a towering inferno! I blow it out
6   and whoosh! It explodes in my face.
7   CORY: Yeah, you looked pretty funny with marshmallow goo all
8   over your face and in your hair. The year of the buzz cut!
9   *(He runs his hand over the top of his friend's head.)*
10 STEPHEN: Don't remind me! *(The two guys laugh as they
11   remember.)*
12 PAIGE: *(Gesturing toward the guys)* Look at them. Laughing and
13   cutting up like two kindergarteners who just heard the
14   word, "underwear."
15 MISTY: Really. I don't think they're mature enough to even be
16   at a dance. Maybe I don't really want to ask Cory to dance
17   after all.
18 PAIGE: You're just getting cold feet. Let them settle back down
19   and then you can make your move.
20 MISTY: I don't know. What if he says no? I'll look stupid walking
21   back over here alone.
22 PAIGE: If he says no, just keep walking. Go to the restroom or
23   something. Or over to the table for a glass of punch. No
24   one will know what you stopped to say to him. You might
25   have been asking the time for all they'll know.
26 MISTY: But *I'll* know. It's too humiliating. I can't risk it.
27 PAIGE: Tell you what. I'll go first. Watch and learn. *(She walks
28   over to the two boys very confidently and then loses her nerve.)*
29   Would you ... um ... could you ... um ... tell me what time
30   it is?
31 STEPHEN: *(Glances at watch.)* Sure ... yeah ... it's seven-thirty ...
32 PAIGE: Oh ... OK ... thanks. *(She turns quickly and walks back
33   to her friend.)*
34 MISTY: What happened? What'd he say?
35 PAIGE: He said it's seven-thirty.

1 MISTY: What? You asked him the time? You didn't even ask him
2   to dance?
3 PAIGE: It just didn't feel right. I don't think he was ready. You
4   have to do things —
5 STEPHEN: — just right. See, that was a classic move. She's
6   letting us know she's interested.
7 CORY: How? She asked you the time! That doesn't mean
8   anything.
9 STEPHEN: That, my friend, means *everything*. Didn't you see
10   her face? All pink and flushed. The girl was definitely
11   flirting.
12 CORY: Flirting? I didn't get that at all. Maybe I'm not ready for
13   all this boy-girl stuff.
14 STEPHEN: Don't go all scared on me now. Those girls made the
15   first move; it's up to us to make the next one.
16 CORY: Sure. They made the easy move. Asking the time ... that
17   is so lame. I don't even think that should count as a move.
18 STEPHEN: Look. It's all a big game. We know it and they know
19   it. See how they keep looking over here at us? They are
20   totally —
21 PAIGE: — staring at us. I knew my plan would work.
22 MISTY: Your plan? I thought your plan was to ask him to dance.
23 PAIGE: No. That's too easy. What you really want is to get *him*
24   to ask *you* to dance.
25 MISTY: But you said —
26 PAIGE: Look, forget what I said. It's all a big game. Kind of like
27   they're the hunter and we're the prey.
28 MISTY: The prey? I don't like the sound of that.
29 PAIGE: See how puffed up they are now? They keep looking over
30   here like a couple of cavemen who are getting ready to drag
31   off their women!
32 MISTY: What? I am definitely *not* going to get dragged anywhere
33   — not in this dress!
34 PAIGE: Great dress, by the way.
35 MISTY: I know! I had to watch my baby sister for three

1   Saturdays straight so that Mom would buy it for me.

2 PAIGE: So worth it!

3 MISTY: I know. I like yours, too. Where'd you get it?

4 PAIGE: Hand–me-down. The price you pay for having an older

5   sister.

6 MISTY: Well, it's still pretty great. And no one would ever know —

7 PAIGE: No one but the teachers. First thing Mr. Gibson said to

8   me was, "You look just as beautiful in that dress as your

9   sister." I was like, "Gee, thanks. Thanks for telling the

10   whole school I'm wearing my sister's dress, Mr. Gibson."

11 MISTY: You said that to him?

12 PAIGE: No, just the first part. But I really wanted to say the

13   other. What is he, a moron?

14 MISTY: I guess guys just don't get how important the dress is.

15 PAIGE: Neither do mothers, apparently.

16 MISTY: Good point. *(Looks over at the guys.)* I don't think the

17   guys are enjoying the whole dress-up thing either.

18 CORY: *(Pulling at his tie)* This thing is choking me!

19 STEPHEN: Me, too. I think my brother tied it too tight on

20   purpose.

21 CORY: Whose idea was it to make this a formal dance? What's

22   wrong with jeans and a T-shirt? That's what I'd like to

23   know.

24 STEPHEN: *(Making a face)* Girls. They love this stuff. Getting all

25   dressed up and acting like a bunch of princesses.

26 CORY: Great. I guess that makes us the princes. Talk about

27   pressure. That's a huge image to live up to.

28 STEPHEN: Look around. I don't see any Prince Charmings

29   hanging out around here. Lucky for us, the girls are stuck

30   with us. So, you about ready?

31 CORY: Uh ... I don't know ...

32 MISTY: What's taking them so long? I don't think they're ever

33   going to come ask us to dance.

34 PAIGE: They will. You'll see. You just have to be patient. Maybe

35   they're waiting for the next slow song. The first song has

1   to be perfect —

2 STEPHEN: Hear that?

3 CORY: What?

4 STPHEN: Slow song. Perfect time to make our move.

5 CORY: OK ... OK ... omigosh ... I don't think I can breathe.

6 STEPHEN: Relax. Just loosen your tie. Take a deep breath. You

7   don't want to appear —

8 PAIGE: — too eager. Take a moment to think about it ... don't

9   rush in and say, "yes!" Here, they come. Now, remember,

10   be patient ... don't rush ...

11 STEPHEN and CORY: Hi girls, would you like to —

12 PAIGE and MISTY: *Yes! Yes, we'd love to!*

Spot and Speck

(2 Guys)
CHARACTERS:
   Seth: Guy who is very full of himself when it comes to girls.
   Trey: Friend who has set Seth up on a blind date.

SETTING:
   Two guys hanging out, getting ready to go meet girls at the movies. Trey has set Seth up on a blind date.

1 SETH: So tell me again what she looks like.

2 TREY: I told you. She's really nice. And she's cute.

3 SETH: Puppy-dog cute or cheerleader cute? 'Cause there's a
4   difference, you know.

5 SETH: Trust me. She's exactly your type.

6 TREY: What do you mean by that? I don't have a type.

7 SETH: Yes, you do. You like short, skinny, blonde, and giggly.
8   Preferably dumb *and* blonde so that you can appear smart.

9 TREY: Hey! That is *so* not true.

10 SETH: *(Counting off on his fingers)* Pam. Angela. Marie.

11 TREY: OK. I see your point. But that doesn't mean I'm not open
12   to change. I would totally be willing to go with a drop-dead
13   brunette with long straight hair and dark brown eyes.

14 SETH: Well, that's pretty open of you.

15 TREY: She could even have more than half a brain. Not too
16   brainy, though. I don't want to be bored to death.

17 SETH: Of course not. But don't worry. Chelsea is definitely not
18   boring.

19 TREY: Oh, no. She's not one of those yappers, is she? You
20   know, the kind who won't shut up for a half a second.

21 SETH: Yappers? Why do you have to make them all sound like
22   dogs?

23 TREY: *(Shrugs.)* I know a lot about dogs. Guess I just think of
24   girls that way too sometimes.

25 SETH: Awesome. That'll make a great first compliment. Tell her
26   she reminds you of a dog. She'll fall in love before the
27   previews are over.

28 TREY: Funny. I'm not dumb enough to actually tell the girl that.

29 SETH: That's good. I'd hate to bring you back home with two
30   black eyes. One from Chelsea and one from Anna. Girls
31   stick together, you know.

32 TREY: Like a pack of dogs. You fight one; you fight them all.

33 SETH: There you go again.

34 TREY: Come on, even you have to admit that one's true.

35 SETH: Maybe. But I'm beginning to see why you don't keep a

1   girlfriend very long.
2 TREY: Too honest?
3 SETH: Too stupid.
4 TREY: Very funny. I do all right. So, answer the question, is she
5   a yapper or not?
6 SETH: She talks the average amount.
7 TREY: Good. Sounds good so far. So what about teeth?
8 SETH: She's got 'em.
9 TREY: Ha ha. You are so funny.
10 SETH: What about her teeth?
11 TREY: Teeth say a lot about a girl.
12 SETH: I'm sure they say a lot about a dog, too, right?
13 TREY: Yeah, but that's not the point. If she has good teeth, that
14   means she takes care of herself.
15 SETH: You seriously want to know about Chelsea's teeth? Was
16   I supposed to have her fill out a questionnaire before
17   tonight? Like, how many times do you brush your teeth?
18   Do you floss regularly? And how about mouthwash? Do you
19   use it? Oh, and braces — are you open to them or do your
20   parents not have a good dental plan?
21 TREY: Make fun. But you know it's true. Gross teeth mean
22   gross breath, and gross breath means gross kissing.
23 SETH: Well, you won't have to worry about that.
24 TREY: Why?
25 SETH: Chelsea is not the kind of girl who would even dream
26   about kissing you tonight.
27 TREY: Why? What's wrong with me?
28 SETH: *(Sarcastically)* Do you want the short list or the long one?
29 TREY: You're a load of laughs. I thought you said she was
30   perfect for me.
31 SETH: She is.
32 TREY: Then why won't she want to kiss me? What did you tell
33   her about me?
34 SETH: Lucky for you, I was very vague when it came to
35   describing you.

1　TREY: *(Sarcastically)* Thanks; you're a real pal. Then why won't
2　　　she kiss me? *(Obviously getting upset)* What kind of
3　　　relationship are we ever going to have if she won't kiss me?
4　SETH: Whoa, boy! Do I need to throw you a bone? One night at
5　　　the movies on a group date, and now you're in a
6　　　relationship?
7　TREY: *(Calming back down)* Well, we could be. You never know.
8　　　But not now. Now that I know she would never even dream
9　　　of kissing me!
10　SETH: Let me put this in terms you'll understand: Put your
11　　　hackles down, boy. I didn't say *never*. I said she wouldn't
12　　　be kissing you tonight.
13　TREY: Why not?
14　SETH: Chelsea is not the kind of girl who kisses a guy on the
15　　　first date. In fact, I doubt she's ever kissed a guy before.
16　　　She takes that kind of stuff seriously.
17　TREY: Oh ... well, that's good. I like that, actually. I wouldn't
18　　　want her going around kissing everybody, like a dog in —
19　SETH: OK! OK! I get it! Enough with the dog phrases!
20　TREY: Sorry. Didn't know you were so sensitive.
21　SETH: I am *not* sensitive. Maybe this was a bad idea. I should've
22　　　never set you up with Chelsea!
23　TREY: Come on. Lighten up! I promise to treat her like royalty.
24　　　*(Pauses and smiles.)* Pamper her like a real show dog!
25　SETH: Stop it!
26　TREY: I'll even bring her a treat, if you want.
27　SETH: Honestly, I don't know how you've *ever* gotten a date
28　　　without my help!
29　TREY: *(Shrugs.)* Girls just dig me.
30　SETH: I sure don't know why. You're like the dog that roams
31　　　around the neighborhood. You know, the mangy mutt type.
32　TREY: So you're allowed to compare me to a dog but I can't
33　　　compare girls to one?
34　SETH: Just trying to use language that you'll understand.
35　TREY: What can I say? Girls like the mangy mutt type

1   apparently.

2 SETH: I'm starting to think I've matched up a poodle with a pit

3   bull.

4 TREY: Poodle? Aw, man. She's not all frilly and made-up, is

5   she? Perfectly manicured? Perfect hair? You know I don't

6   like high-maintenance girls.

7 SETH: I promise you, she is not perfect.

8 TREY: But she does try, right? I mean, she does put forth *some*

9   effort in the makeup and hair department, right?

10 SETH: Have I ever told you how impossible you are?

11 TREY: About three times today already.

12 SETH: Well, count this as the fourth.

13 TREY: You can't blame a guy for knowing what he likes. I'm sure

14   Chelsea's doing the same thing. Sitting around pumping

15   Anna for information about me.

16 SETH: Let's hope not, or you'll be getting the "Something's

17   come up" phone call any minute.

18 TREY: Nah, they're probably trying on sixteen different outfits

19   trying to decide what to wear.

20 SETH: If I know Anna, she'll have the normal blue jeans and

21   hoodie on.

22 TREY: What about Chelsea? What do you think she'll wear?

23 SETH: Probably jeans and some kind of girlie shirt. She doesn't

24   seem the type to wear a hoodie out on a date.

25 TREY: Cool. I like that. So what are you wearing?

26 SETH: *(Clearly offended)* What do you mean, what am I wearing?

27   I'm wearing this. *(Gestures to what he has on.)* That's what

28   I'm wearing.

29 TREY: Really. You're wearing that.

30 SETH: Yeah. What's wrong with it?

31 TREY: *(Brushes at his shoulder.)* Dude, you got a little something

32   on the shoulder there.

33 SETH: *(Looks down at it.)* Crud. Where'd that come from?

34 TREY: I don't know, but it looks pretty bad.

35 SETH: Yeah. Anna will flip. She hates it if I wear something

1   crumpled or dirty looking.

2 TREY: Who wouldn't?

3 SETH: *(Still looking at it)* I guess I'm going to have to change.

4 TREY: I would. People might stare otherwise. They'll be like,

5   "Dude, you ever hear of a napkin?"

6 SETH: Come on. It's not that bad. In fact, now that I really look

7   at it, I don't think Anna will even notice.

8 TREY: You're kidding, right? It's like a car wreck! It's like, bam!

9   There it is! And then you can't take your eyes off it.

10 SETH: Now you're just exaggerating. It's barely a speck.

11 TREY: A speck? Dude, it's huge.

12 SETH: What? What about you? Look at that! *(Points to TREY's*

13   *shirt.)*

14 TREY: *(Looks down at a huge spot.)* This? Oh, this is nothing.

15 SETH: Nothing? Are you crazy, man?

16 TREY: I don't even think anyone will notice.

17 SETH: Are you kidding me? You're like a walking bull's-eye!

18 TREY: I think you're being a little overdramatic, don't you? I

19   mean, it practically blends in.

20 SETH: Blends in with what?

21 TREY: It's nothing like that *thing* on your shoulder. It's like a

22   neon sign saying, "Look at me! Look at me!"

23 SETH: What? You're comparing this little speck on my shoulder

24   to that huge spot on your shirt?

25 TREY: Just trying to be your friend, man.

26 SETH: So you're allowed to look like a mangy mutt, but I'm not?

27 TREY: It doesn't work for everybody, dude.

28 SETH: It doesn't work for you!

29 TREY: Sure it does. I bet you anything that Chelsea won't say a

30   word about it.

31 SETH: Of course not! It's your first date. She'll be too

32   embarrassed to mention it!

33 TREY: Well, there you go. It's the perfect shirt for a first date

34   then.

35 SETH: Not if you're wanting to get a second date.

1   TREY: Hey, if you start the relationship out with low
2   expectations, then the only way to go is up.
3   SETH: What relationship?!
4   TREY: The one Chelsea and I are going to have.
5   SETH: You are unbelievable!
6   TREY: I know.
7   SETH: It *wasn't* a compliment.
8   TREY: Maybe not to you. That's why you need to change your
9   shirt. Like I said, you can't handle being the mangy mutt.
10 SETH: *(Sighs heavily.)* Look. Just give me a shirt — a clean one
11   — to borrow, OK?

Locker Room Smack

(3 Guys)
CHARACTERS:

Chad: Basketball player who wants to quit after he sees the other team.

Vince: Basketball player who also wants to throw in the towel; afraid of being embarrassed.

Hunter: Basketball player who also is intimidated but tries to be optimistic; temporary captain.

SETTING:

Locker room before the big game. Star player is out. Other team has some very intimidating players; they look like giants. The guys are very dejected and ready to give up. Hunter takes his new role as temporary captain seriously and tries to rally the team.

1 VINCE: We might as well hand over the trophy now.

2 CHAD: For real. Did you see those guys as they got off the bus?

3 VINCE: They're giants! Real live giants!

4 HUNTER: One of them actually hit his head on the roof! The
5   roof of the bus! Do you *know* how tall that is?

6 VINCE: It's gotta be close to eight feet!

7 HUNTER: Come on, there's no way the guy was eight feet tall!

8 CHAD: Well, a good six feet then! The guy was taller than my
9   dad! Have you seen my dad? They didn't call him "Flag
10   Pole" in high school for nothing.

11 VINCE: So where'd you get your height from? Your mom? Or
12   your little sister?

13 CHAD: Funny. I just haven't had my growth spurt yet. It's
14   coming. Believe me, it's coming.

15 HUNTER: Well, if you could get that to come — like right now —
16   that'd be great!

17 CHAD: No one's supposed to be that tall at our age. It's unnatural.

18 CHAD: Yeah. These guys must have all flunked a couple of grades!

19 VINCE: Really. There's no way they're supposed to be in middle
20   school.

21 HUNTER: Coach needs to check their records. The school
22   probably brought their high school — or college — team to
23   beat us!

24 CHAD: You think maybe they're taking steroids or something?

25 HUNTER: Steroids don't make you taller — just more muscular.

26 VINCE: Well, they've got that going on, too. Did you see the
27   guns on number twenty-three? He's going to pulverize us!

28 CHAD: Number three was pretty ripped, too. He was practically
29   splitting out the front of his jersey. Like the Hulk.

30 VINCE: *(Groaning.)* We are so dead.

31 HUNTER: Maybe we can just let them all foul out.

32 CHAD: You think we could survive a foul by one of them? We'll
33   lose our whole team to injuries!

34 VINCE: Chad's right. We haven't got a chance! Especially not
35   without Rick!

1   CHAD: I can't believe he hurt his ankle this week! *This week!*

2   HUNTER: Coach said he's out for the rest of the season.

3   CHAD: After tonight, we'll *all* be out for the season.

4   VINCE: Maybe we should just save ourselves the embarrassment

5   and quit now.

6   HUNTER: Come on. We might be small, but we're not quitters.

7   VINCE: I am *not* small. I may not be gargantuan like those apes,

8   but I am not small!

9   CHAD: My girlfriend is going to be out there. I don't want to look

10   like a fool in front of her.

11   HUNTER: *(Trying to ease the situation)* Why should tonight be any

12   different?

13   CHAD: Very funny. The only reason you don't care as much is

14   because you warm the bench half the time anyway. You'll

15   be safe sitting on the sidelines!

16   HUNTER: I do not! Who made three baskets last game?

17   VINCE: Ooooh! Three whole baskets? Wow! We should've

18   dedicated the game ball to you!

19   HUNTER: It's not my job to take the shots — it's yours! I'm

20   supposed to block.

21   CHAD: Well, good luck with that tonight! I want to see you try

22   to block one of those animals!

23   VINCE: We're going to be the laughingstock of the whole school

24   after this.

25   HUNTER: Come on. Maybe they're tall and dumb. Maybe they

26   can't even dribble with those big long legs.

27   CHAD: Now you're dreaming.

28   HUNTER: Think about giraffes. All tall and clumsy. Maybe

29   they've all got two left feet.

30   VINCE: So what if they do? They'll still be able to push right

31   past us!

32   CHAD: Yeah, call me crazy, but *I'm* not getting in their way.

33   HUNTER: So we'll go around them. We'll be fast and quick —

34   like bees buzzing around their heads.

35   VINCE: *(Shaking his head in disbelief)* You're going to end up like

1   a bug smashed on a car windshield.

2 HUNTER: Listen. Every team has to have a weakness. What if

3   they can't even shoot the ball?

4 VINCE: They don't need to shoot; they can just stand there and

5   drop it in.

6 CHAD: I bet they could just play three players and still beat us.

7 VINCE: With their hands tied behind their backs.

8 HUNTER: If Rick were here, he wouldn't be letting you talk like

9   this.

10 CHAD: Well, Rick's not here, is he?

11 HUNTER: You're just letting them get in your head. We all are.

12   We need to focus on the positive instead of panicking.

13 VINCE: What positive?

14 HUNTER: Well, for one, we are undefeated this season.

15 CHAD: Big whoop. We've only played two games.

16 HUNTER: And won them both.

17 VINCE: One team didn't even have uniforms. I think it was the

18   school's first year to even have a basketball team.

19 CHAD: I'd hardly call that a huge victory, Hunter.

20 HUNTER: But our last game was close. Remember that?

21 CHAD: Yeah. And we had Rick! Our captain. Our star player.

22   Without him, we wouldn't even be able to win against a

23   normal, non-giant-sized team!

24 HUNTER: That's not true! You guys know it takes more than

25   one person to make a winning team. We all have a role. A

26   responsibility. We just have to work together —

27 VINCE: Is this your idea of a pep talk? *(Pause)* Wait a minute!

28   Did coach make you captain?

29 HUNTER: *(Looking down like he doesn't want to tell them)* Well, he

30   might have said something about temporary —

31 VINCE: You? Captain?! That's not fair! I've been playing ball two

32   more years than you!

33 CHAD: *(To VINCE)* And I've been playing two more years than

34   *you!* *(To HUNTER)* Why would coach make you captain?

35 HUNTER: Hey! What's wrong with me being captain? I might not

1   have played ball as long as either of you, but I'm just as
2   good a ball player.

3 VINCE: You wish! You can't even slam-dunk!

4 CHAD: I can dribble circles around you!

5 HUNTER: Well, maybe being a captain is about more than
6   playing ball!

7 VINCE: Maybe, if you're captain of the chess club or the swim
8   team, but being captain of this team means it's *all* about
9   playing ball.

10 CHAD: You have to live, eat, and breathe basketball to be a
11   captain.

12 HUNTER: Really? Is that why you were ready to quit a minute
13   ago? Because you live, eat, and breathe basketball?

14 CHAD: I was just caught up in the fear ... but fear makes a
15   player great! Did you know that? Huh, Mr. Captain? Did you
16   know that?

17 VINCE: ... and I was just trying to pump us up ... get us ready
18   for the big game!

19 HUNTER: You call that pumping us up? Weren't you the one that
20   wanted to hand over the win? Without even trying?

21 VINCE: It was just a figure of speech. I was hoping you guys
22   would get mad! Become the fighters that I know you can be!

23 HUNTER: Yeah, right. Don't even try to be motivational now! If
24   you were temporary captain, we would've quit fifteen
25   minutes ago.

26 CHAD: Really, Vince. You're so full of bull. You took one look at
27   those guys and came running in here like a dog with his tail
28   in between his legs.

29 HUNTER: That's it! *(Says this loudly as if he's just gotten an idea.)*

30 VINCE: What? What's it?

31 HUNTER: They're so tall; we'll just run in between their legs!

32 VINCE: *(Laughing)* What is that saying? The bigger you are, the
33   harder you fall?

34 CHAD: Then we're in for one heck of an earthquake if one of
35   those dudes hits the ground!

1 HUNTER: We just need a strategy.

2 VINCE: *(Teasing)* And quitting isn't a strategy?

3 HUNTER and CHAD: *No!*

4 VINCE: Just kidding. I'm willing to go get pulverized if you guys are.

5 HUNTER: So what else have we got? We need some secret
6   weapons! An ace in the hole!

7 CHAD: My girlfriend's pretty hot; I can have her try to distract
8   them!

9 VINCE: Awesome! Just don't let her distract *you!*

10 HUNTER: We could douse ourselves in really strong body spray.
11   They'll be gagging so much, they won't be able to play!

12 CHAD: Killer! What else have we got?

13 VINCE: When they're sitting on the bench, I'll distract them and
14   you sneak under their chairs and tie their shoelaces
15   together!

16 CHAD: No way! They'd kill me if they saw me!

17 VINCE: Glue on the soles of their shoes?

18 HUNTER: Or maybe on the basketball! We'll never get to touch
19   it anyway!

20 CHAD: I know! We'll turn the heat up in the gym! Bodies that
21   big are sure to get hot quick. They'll be passing out in no
22   time!

23 VINCE: Sure, after they've sweated a river for us to drown in!

24 HUNTER: Maybe we can reduce the oxygen in the room — the
25   air's got to be thinner way up where they are!

26 CHAD: I say we pants them! Can you imagine those guys with
27   their shorts around their ankles?

28 VINCE: Uh, no. Thank goodness. But I can imagine what your
29   face would look like if you so much as went near their
30   pants.

31 CHAD: Good point.

32 HUNTER: I've got it! What about their academic records?
33   There's no way those monster jocks have the required
34   GPAs to play! We just need to call their school and get
35   them disqualified!

1 VINCE: We don't have time! Didn't you just hear the buzzer? It's
2   time for us to take the gym and warm up!
3 CHAD: *(Getting serious)* **Well, guys.** *(Pats them on the back.)* **It's**
4   **been nice knowing you.**
5 VINCE: I'll really miss you guys. Tell my family that I love them.
6 HUNTER: What makes you think we'll survive?
7 VINCE: Well, they'll obviously go after me.
8 CHAD: You? Why?
9 VINCE: Star player. You know. Take out the leader and the rest
10   will fall.
11 CHAD: Star player? *Leader?* Since when did you become either
12   one of those?
13 VINCE: *(Patting him on the back)* **Come on, dude. You know it's true.**
14 CHAD: It is not! Who got MVP last year? Oh yeah. That's right.
15   Me! If they're going to take anyone out, it's going to be me!
16 HUNTER: You? What about me? I'm the captain —
17 CHAD: *Temporary* captain —
18 HUNTER: They're going to zero in and demolish me. Without a
19   captain, the team is sure to fall apart! *(The three guys walk*
20   *off still arguing — "yeah, right." "Well, we'll just see won't we?")*

Battle of the Voices

(2 Guys, 1 Girl)
CHARACTERS:

Gus: Fan of Curt, the hard-core singer.

Brad: Also a fan of Curt; doesn't like Amber's favorite singer.

Amber: Thinks Daniel is the best singer and is glad that Curt got voted off.

SETTING:

Sitting around (could be one of their houses) talking about the national singing show results from the night before.

1 GUS: There's no way Curt should have gone home last night.
2 It's completely bogus.
3 BRAD: For real. They kept that hoarse sounding guy who forgot
4 his lines and got rid of Curt? It's completely rigged.
5 AMBER: Hey, America voted. And America says Curt is gone! I
6 think America got it right!
7 GUS: You would.
8 BRAD: You just didn't like Curt because of his hair.
9 AMBER: Well, it sure didn't help! How could I possibly think of
10 him as a star with nasty hair like that!
11 BRAD: It's not supposed to be about the hair, it's supposed to
12 be about the singing.
13 AMBER: Exactly. His nasally sounding voice got on my nerves.
14 His songs made me want to vomit.
15 BRAD: Daniel's songs make me want to vomit! All gushy junk.
16 He might as well be a girl.
17 AMBER: Please. Who even knows what Curt sings about; you
18 can't even understand him! It's just a bunch of screaming
19 and stuff! Most of the time I just plug my ears when he
20 comes On-stage!
21 GUS: That's just because you don't know what good music is.
22 If it's not some slow song about love, you don't want to
23 hear it.
24 AMBER: How are you supposed to sing along if you can't even
25 understand the lyrics?
26 GUS: Sing along? What are you — in kindergarten? You don't
27 sing along to songs like Curt sings. You just sit back and
28 enjoy them.
29 BRAD: *(Throwing head up and down)* And maybe do a little head
30 banging — like this!
31 AMBER: All that does is give me a headache. Like Curt's music!
32 BRAD: Well, your precious Daniel's going to be the next to go.
33 He can't possibly last much longer. He forgot his lyrics!
34 What kind of a star does that?
35 GUS: For real. Never been to a concert before where the singer

103

1   was like, "Whoa! Wait up. I forgot the words. Can we start

2   again?"

3 AMBER: Who would know if Curt forgot his lyrics? He doesn't

4   even sing any! And Daniel forgetting his lyrics just made

5   him seem more real. More humble.

6 BRAD: What else could he be but humble? Dude forgets his

7   lyrics. I doubt he's going to be strutting around the place.

8 AMBER: It doesn't matter what he sings — right or wrong words

9   — he's still way better than Curt. Obviously.

10 GUS: The vote last night doesn't prove anything! It just shows

11   America's biased — like you!

12 BRAD: I'm so sick of the judges saying that Daniel could sing

13   the phone book and people would listen! Just shows they

14   don't have a clue about real talent either!

15 GUS: It's more of a popularity contest than anything. People

16   don't care what the contestants sound like. They just vote

17   based on who's cute and who isn't.

18 AMBER: So not true. Have you seen the past winners? At least

19   three of them are plain — if not downright ugly.

20 GUS: That was the beauty of the show before all of America

21   started watching it. Now it's just so predictable.

22 BRAD: For real. Cute. Great personality. Doesn't matter if you

23   can't sing, we're going to vote for you anyway.

24 AMBER: What about last year? That old guy won! You think that

25   was a popularity contest?

26 GUS: I don't know *what* that was. But have you heard of him

27   since? No. Obviously America got it wrong on that one.

28   He's faded into oblivion.

29 BRAD: I just want to know what would happen if they only

30   allowed one vote per person. That would sure change

31   everything!

32 GUS: No more non-stop texting votes from lovesick girls like

33   you! Then those teenage boys who can't sing — like Daniel

34   — wouldn't have a chance.

35 AMBER: I think that just proves how great they are. We're

1   dedicated and loyal fans. Just imagine if we voted for the
2   President that way. We'd have the guy ... or girl ... who the
3   public *really* loved.
4 GUS: What? No we wouldn't. We'd have some hot guy that all
5   the teenage girls loved! Probably wouldn't have a brain in
6   his head either, much less the experience to be President.
7 AMBER: So you think I'm incapable of voting for a good candidate?
8 GUS: Exactly. I can just hear you now. *(Mocking)* Ewwww ... I
9   wouldn't vote for him. Look at his hair! How can we
10   possibly have a president with hair like that?
11 BRAD: *(Mocking)* Ooooh ... or clothes like that! I wouldn't be
12   able to look at him wearing something so ... nerdy!
13 AMBER: You guys are a real hoot. I can just see who we would
14   get if it were left up to you. A gun-toting Amazon-type man
15   who would start more wars than we have countries to fight
16   with!
17 GUS: Well, we could use a guy with a little more guts, that's for sure.
18 BRAD: Yeah! We need a guy who will stand up to people. Show
19   other countries exactly what America is made of! Stop
20   acting like a girl and be a man!
21 AMBER: See what I mean? You're no different! You wouldn't
22   vote on the issues, you'd vote for some macho maniac.
23   Like Curt, just because you thought he was cool with that
24   funky, nasty hair!
25 GUS: At least he dressed like a star! Your guy looks like he
26   should be doing taxes or something! He'll never make it
27   dressed like that!
28 AMBER: I thought you said it was about the singing. What does
29   it matter what he wears?
30 GUS: Just saying ... if you think the public is going to vote for
31   him; you're crazy.
32 AMBER: Well, they voted for him last night, didn't they?
33 BRAD: They're going to get tired of his "I'm so humble" attitude
34   real quick. A star has to be confident and sure of himself.
35 AMBER: Really? 'Cause your boy's over-confident attitude got

1   him voted right off the stage, didn't it? America doesn't
2   want some puffed-up male diva winning the show.
3   GUS: Male diva? Are you kidding me? I read somewhere that
4   Daniel demands fresh-squeezed lemonade — at a certain
5   temperature — every day before practice.
6   AMBER: Lemons are good for your vocal chords. That's not
7   being a diva, that's being smart! And I heard that Curt
8   demanded *only* red M&Ms in a bowl on his dressing table.
9   BRAD: That's just quirky. Not diva-ish.
10 AMBER: And that he makes the cameras only shoot his left side
11   so that everyone can see that stupid scar running down his
12   cheek. It's probably fake, too.
13 GUS: That's his trademark. He's making sure everyone
14   recognizes him.
15 BRAD: Yeah, like Marilyn Monroe.
16 GUS: Or Cindy Crawford.
17 BRAD: Or Donald Trump's hair! To be famous you have to have
18   a trademark!
19 AMBER: That's funny. I thought it was about the singing.
20   Shouldn't a great voice be his trademark? If he had one.
21 GUS: We'll never know, now will we? Since finicky America
22   voted him out.
23 BRAD: Oh, he'll be a star anyway. They'd be crazy not to snatch
24   him up.
25 AMBER: He's had his fifteen minutes of fame. I hope he enjoyed
26   them!
27 GUS: You are so wrong! I bet he'll have an album out by the end
28   of the year.
29 BRAD: And I'll be the first one in line to buy it!
30 AMBER: You'll be the only one in line to buy it!
31 GUS: Your guy will probably be singing in a karaoke bar or playing
32   a character at a theme park musical before it's all over.
33 AMBER: You are so off-base. He's going to win the whole thing
34   and be a mega-star!
35 GUS: Maybe he'll sing kiddie songs for children's shows.

1 BRAD: Or jingles for commercials.

2 GUS: Or — I know! — He'll become a soap star! I can see it
3 now, long-lost son finally introduced to dear old Dad on a
4 heart-wrenching, cliff-hanging episode of some lame
5 daytime soap!

6 BRAD: Or he could sell hair products! You know that fifties style
7 is bound to come back one day!

8 GUS: Wait! I've got a better idea! He can star in a horror movie
9 about nerdy boys gone bad! He'll stab people to death with
10 his mechanical pencil!

11 BRAD: Or kill them with his singing!

12 GUS: Oh yeah! Now *that* would be torture!

13 AMBER: You guys are a real comedy routine.

14 GUS and BRAD: *(Nudging each other and laughing, clearly pleased*
15 *with themselves)* We are, aren't we?

16 BRAD: *(Suddenly jumps up.)* I've got the best idea! If America
17 loves Daniel, they'll love you, Gus! *(Pulls him up, too.)*

18 GUS: What?

19 BRAD: You should totally try out, dude!

20 GUS: I *have* always loved singing!

21 AMBER: Give me a break!

22 BRAD: Come on. Sing us some tunes! You know you've got to
23 be better than Daniel! *(GUS uses hand as a mic and starts*
24 *singing badly. Can sing the lyrics of any popular love song —*
25 *clearly making fun of the situation to AMBER. BRAD claps and*
26 *encourages.)* Awesome, dude! You rock! You sound just like
27 Daniel, man! I can see your name in lights already!

28 GUS: *(Acts like he's handing mic to BRAD.)* Your turn, dude! Rock
29 it out! *(BRAD starts belting out a tune. GUS can chime in, too.*
30 *AMBER watches for a minute, clearly disgusted, shaking her*
31 *head, rolling her eyes.)*

32 AMBER: *(Loudly, over BRAD's singing)* I'm out of here. You guys
33 clearly don't know a great singer when you hear one!

What's Her Name?

(3 Guys)

CHARACTERS:

Justin: Guy who likes to date a lot of girls. Goes from one relationship to another quickly.

Cameron: Friend who is tired of waiting for Justin to wrap up his call to his girlfriend. Finds out he is dating the same girl. He is the first to break it off with her.

Jonathan: Another friend who is also tired of Justin's lengthy phone call. He also finds out that he's dating the same girl.

SETTING:

The three guys are over at Justin's house. Justin is on the phone with his new girlfriend.

1   JUSTIN: No, I love you more. No, really. You can't love me more,
2   because I love you *so* much. I miss you too.
3   CAMERON: *(To JONATHAN)* Not again. Who is it this week?
4   Wasn't it just Leslie?
5   JONATHAN: Dude, where have you been? That was like two
6   weeks ago. I think he went with a girl named Alicia after
7   that!
8   CAMERON: *(Sarcastically)* Sorry. I don't keep up with Justin's
9   girlfriends.
10 CAMERON: Who can?
11 JUSTIN: No, I really love you more. You could never love me
12   more, 'cause I love you more than anything and you can't
13   love someone more than that.
14 CAMERON: Get off the phone already!
15 JUSTIN: OK, I gotta go. I'll call you in a few minutes. I love you
16   soooo much! I'll miss you so much. I'll think of you every
17   minute until we talk again. I'll be counting the minutes that
18   we aren't talking. I love you. *(Makes kissing noises into*
19   *phone.)*
20 CAMERON: Finally! Gosh, we can actually do something now!
21 JUSTIN: No, I'll miss you more ... *(JONATHAN grabs the phone*
22   *out of JUSTIN's hands and hangs up.)* Hey! *(Tries to grab phone*
23   *back.)*
24 CAMERON: Give it a rest, OK?
25 JUSTIN: Why would you do that? Now I have to call her back
26   and tell her that you hung up on her. She'll think I did it!
27   Oh, man, I hope she's not mad!
28 JONATHAN: I think she'll live.
29 CAMERON: We're ready to play video games or something, not
30   listen to you go on about how much you love and miss this
31   girl.
32 JONATHAN: Dude, you've been on the phone all day.
33 JUSTIN: And if it wasn't for you, I'd be on there for two days. I
34   could talk to her all week. She's awesome. She's so
35   amazing. I can talk to her about anything.

1 JONATHAN: Yeah, I heard you the first seven times. What
2   happened with Leslie anyway? Just two weeks ago you
3   were in love with her.
4 JUSTIN: Leslie? Don't you mean Alicia ... oh wait ... I guess
5   Leslie was right before that ...
6 CAMERON: You can't even keep them straight. You were with
7   Leslie at least a month — almost a record for you. What
8   happened to her?
9 JUSTIN: She got way too clingy. She wanted to hang out with
10   me all the time. That got annoying real fast. Then, she kept
11   saying that she loved me like every two seconds.
12 CAMERON: Hmmmm. That sounds like somebody I know.
13   Somebody really close to me who calls his new girlfriend
14   every five seconds.
15 JUSTIN: Newsflash, *she* called *me* and wanted to talk. What am
16   I going to do? Say no? To a great girl like her? I don't think
17   so!
18 CAMERON: Dude, you move on way too fast.
19 JONATHAN: So, who is she? You've been talking to her — and
20   about her — all day and haven't even said her name. I want
21   to know. Is she somebody at school?
22 JUSTIN: You wouldn't know her. I met her at my aunt's who
23   lives an hour away. We met over a week ago and I got her
24   number. We've been talking ever since.
25 CAMERON: What? Did you go through all the girls around here?
26 JUSTIN: Very funny. This girl is so amazing. She's like the
27   perfect girl for me.
28 JONATHAN: So you keep saying. *(Pause)* That's weird. My
29   girlfriend lives an hour away too.
30 CAMERON: Hey, mine does, too. *(Pause)* I guess all the great
31   girls live out of town, huh? *(Joking)* Maybe we should start
32   a club or something!
33 JUSTIN: Well, no one can beat mine. She's great. She plays
34   softball, she gets all A's, and she's really hot. *(CAMERON*
35   *and JONATHAN laugh.)*

1 JUSTIN: What? You don't believe me? You're probably just
2   jealous.
3 JONATHAN: Well, just looking at your past girlfriends, it
4   wouldn't surprise me if this girl was the biggest nerd in the
5   school. Just look at Leslie: major teacher's pet. Knows all
6   the answers. Never does anything wrong. You dated her, so
7   there's no telling what you think is hot.
8 JUSTIN: Leslie wasn't the teacher's pet. She was just a good
9   student who liked her teachers and they liked her back. Is
10   there a problem with being a good student?
11 CAMERON: To cheat off of, no. To date, yes.
12 JONATHAN: Yeah, for real. You like your friends — who are girls
13   — to have brains. Not your girlfriends.
14 JUSTIN: She really wasn't that smart if you think about it.
15 JONATHAN: Are we talking about the same person? Captain of
16   the BETA club, Academic team officer, President of the
17   Student Council, plays no sports, unless you count the
18   Leader of the Science Club as a sport. Plus, she brings the
19   teachers muffins every morning. *(Sarcastically)* You're right.
20   She definitely wasn't a nerd.
21 JUSTIN: Well, that doesn't matter now because I broke up with
22   her a long while ago.
23 JONATHAN: What? It was like a week or two ago. How is that
24   a long while ago?
25 CAMERON: In Justin's head, a week is like a month when it
26   comes to who he broke up with.
27 JUSTIN: I'm over her anyway. I moved on.
28 CAMERON: Well, I don't think she did. Have you seen her blog
29   on Myspace? Can you say "obsessed"?
30 JONATHAN: *(Imitating LESLIE)* "Oh, Justin, I'm so sorry. I'll do
31   anything to be with you again. I've never gone out with
32   anyone like you. Well, actually you're the only person I've
33   gone out with. I love you. You're amazing. I'm so sorry for
34   whatever I did." There's like seven pages of how sorry she
35   is. Even if you're not over her, I think she'll love you forever.

1   *(Both JONATHAN and CAMERON "Awwww" sarcastically.)*
2 JUSTIN: What are you guys — three? Anyway, I'm over her for
3   good. I've moved on and will never go back to her.
4 CAMERON: Are you sure? You said that about Stephanie, too,
5   after the fourth time you went out. You probably still aren't
6   over Stephanie and you'll probably be back to Leslie.
7   *(CAMERON and JONATHAN laugh.)*
8 JUSTIN: I am over her. I have Alexis. Alexis and I aren't going
9   to be like that. We're going to be together forever, I know it.
10 JONATHAN: What did you say her name was? Alexis?
11 JUSTIN: Yeah. What's wrong with that? Gosh, is this about the
12   Alexis I went out with in sixth grade, because that was a
13   long time ago.
14 JONATHAN: No, it's just ... Never mind. It's nothing.
15 CAMERON: Hold on, you said she lives an hour away and her
16   name is Alexis? That's weird.
17 JUSTIN: What? What's weird?
18 JONATHAN: Does she like to be called Lexi?
19 JUSTIN: Hey. How did you know that?
20 CAMERON and JONATHAN: *I'm* dating Lexi! *(All of the guys look*
21   *at each other, confused.)*
22 JUSTIN: Well, it can't be *my* Lexi; she would never cheat on me.
23   She's too good for that. What's her last name?
24 CAMERON: Morris.
25 JONATHAN: Uh oh, her last name is Morris, too.
26 JUSTIN: What?! How could you guys do this to me? I finally find
27   the perfect girlfriend and you guys are trying to steal her.
28   Don't play games with me; I love this girl.
29 CAMERON: We aren't playing with you! Anyway, it's not like she
30   told me she had two other boyfriends.
31 JUSTIN: How do you guys even know her?
32 CAMERON: When there was a girl's softball match out of town
33   and I had to go watch my sister play. I guess her team was
34   playing Lexi's sister's, too. It was really boring because my
35   sister wasn't even playing. So, I went to go get something

1   at the concession stand and she was in line in front of me
2   and we started talking.
3   JONATHAN: Hey, I went to that game and I met Lexi there too.
4   I didn't see you anywhere.
5   JUSTIN: Well, I'm not breaking up with her, I love her. You guys
6   have to.
7   CAMERON: What? No way. *(They both look at JONATHAN.)*
8   JONATHAN: I'm definitely not. She's great.
9   JUSTIN: I guess you guys are going to have to live without her.
10   She's mine.
11   CAMERON: Oh, why don't you just go back to Leslie!
12   JUSTIN: Well, two of us have to dump Lexi, and we all know it
13   isn't me, so ...
14   JONATHAN: What if we all break up with her?
15   CAMERON: Yeah, then she can see how we feel.
16   CAMERON: I'll go first. *(Gets out his cell phone and dials Lexi's*
17   *number.)* Hey! We need to talk. *(Pause.)* Uhh, I think we need
18   to just be friends. *(Pause.)* Probably because you're
19   cheating on me with my two best friends! *(CAMERON hangs*
20   *up the phone, really angry.)* That felt good. I can't stand
21   people like that. If I would've known earlier, I would've
22   never asked her out.
23   JONATHAN: My turn. *(Takes out his phone and dials Lexi's*
24   *number.)* Hey. I've got something to tell you. We're over! *(He*
25   *hangs up, really mad.)* Some girls make me really mad,
26   especially girls like that. It's like they think they can do
27   whatever they want and not get caught, and when they do
28   get caught, they act all innocent.
29   JUSTIN: Well now, she only has me!
30   CAMERON and JONATHAN: No, it's your turn!
31   JUSTIN: OK, OK. I'm going. Gosh, this is gonna stink. I can't
32   believe I'm gonna break up with the best girlfriend I've ever
33   had. She's so wonderful and ...
34   JONATHAN: *(Interrupting)* OK, we get it; let's just get it over
35   with. *(JUSTIN grabs his phone and dials Lexi's number.)*

1   JUSTIN: Hey baby! I'm really sorry, but we have to break up. I'm
2   sorry. But I can't date someone when I'm not the only
3   person. *(Hangs up. He looks like he's about to cry.)*
4   JONATHAN: This night stunk. I'm done with girls like that. I
5   thought she was great until this. She probably lied about
6   other stuff too. I'm glad we're done with her. Well, I have
7   to get home. My mom said I had to be home like two hours
8   ago, so I guess I won't see you guys for a while. Call me
9   later.
10   CAMERON: Yeah. Me too. I have to be home in a few minutes
11   anyway. We should do this again, except without the
12   backstabbing girls. They're so annoying. I'm glad we broke
13   up with her. She could've ruined our friendship. Well, I'm
14   going. *(Walks to one side of the stage then stops. JONATHAN*
15   *walks to opposite side of the stage and then stops. JUSTIN*
16   *smiles really big. He grabs his phone.)*
17   JUSTIN: Hey Lexi! Sorry I hung up on you so fast earlier. I miss
18   you, too. I really, really love you.
19   CAMERON: *(When JUSTIN is finished speaking)* Hey, Lexi. About
20   that call earlier ... I was just kidding. You know I love you
21   baby ...
22   JONATHAN: *(When CAMERON is finished speaking)* Hi, baby! I'm
23   sorry about earlier. You know I was just playing. That's
24   me. Class clown, right? Anyway, can you go out Friday
25   night?

The BB Gun Incident

(4 Guys)
CHARACTERS:

Jacob: Guy who was too afraid to fire his BB gun. Knows for sure that he didn't shoot Wes in the eye by accident.

Keith: Doesn't see the point in trying to figure out who did it because knowing won't change the outcome.

Mason: Upset about Wes but afraid of getting in trouble.

Tanner: Accuses Jacob of lying. Tends to panic a lot about the situation.

SETTING:

The four guys are sitting around talking. They are upset that their friend Wes has lost one of his eyes from a BB gun pellet. One of them did it. They just don't know which one.

1   KEITH: I don't get what the big deal is.

2   JACOB: Wes loses his eye and you don't think it's a big deal?

3   KEITH: Of course that's big. But why does it matter who did it?

4   It's not going to change anything. It's not going to give Wes

5   his eyeball back.

6   MASON: I guess he just wants to know. Wants somebody to

7   fess up.

8   TANNER: How are we supposed to know? It was dark. The BBs

9   were flying. Could have been any one of us.

10 KEITH: Really. It was crazy that night. How are we supposed to

11   know for sure what happened?

12 MASON: I got three welts on my legs. It's not like I could tell

13   you who shot me either.

14 TANNER: I know. It was so dark. I couldn't see anything.

15 KEITH: There's no way to know who shot Wes.

16 JACOB: I know it wasn't me.

17 MASON: What? How can you know? We were all there! Same

18   time. Same place. It could've been any one of us.

19 TANNER: Really. We all had the same kind of guns. Same BBs.

20   The one that hit Wes could've come from any of us.

21 JACOB: Look. I *know* it didn't come from mine.

22 MASON: What are you? Pyschic?

23 KEITH: Did you have some kind of dream where you saw who

24   did it? And you just happen to not be it? How convenient!

25 TANNER: Really. You just don't want to feel guilty like the rest

26   of us. Wondering if it was you who did it.

27 JACOB: I know it wasn't me because I never fired my gun.

28 MASON: What? You're lying! We *all* fired our guns!

29 JACOB: I didn't.

30 KEITH: Why not? Why would you be out there playing war with

31   us and not firing your gun? That would be idiotic!

32 JACOB: *(Looking embarrassed)* I was afraid.

33 MASON: Afraid? Of what? The BBs? They sting a little, but

34   they're completely harmless.

35 JACOB: Really? Tell that to Wes.

1 MASON: Oh. Yeah. Well, that's just a freak accident. We've
2   done it before and no one got hurt.
3 KEITH: Everything's fun until somebody loses an eye.
4 JACOB: Dude! That is so not funny!
5 KEITH: Sorry. It's just something my mom always says and it
6   just popped into my head.
7 MASON: *(To JACOB)* So you didn't fire your gun at all? Not even
8   once?
9 JACOB: No. Not one single time.
10 TANNER: What'd you do the whole time?
11 JACOB: *(Looking away)* Nothing.
12 MASON: He's lying. Look at his face!
13 TANNER: Really! Why you turning so red, Jacob? What'd you do
14   that night if you weren't firing your gun at us?
15 JACOB: *(Obviously embarrassed and upset)* I hid, OK? I found a
16   great hiding spot and I stayed in it the whole time. I didn't
17   come out. Not one time!
18 KEITH: You hid? Like a little girl? Crouched under some bushes
19   afraid of your own shadow?
20 MASON: Is Jacob afraid of the dark? Did Jacob need his teddy
21   bear? Or his Mommy?
22 TANNER: We should've known you weren't man enough to play.
23 JACOB: Say what you want. At least I've got both of my eyes
24   *and* I'm not eaten up with guilt thinking that I hurt Wes! I
25   don't have to face his parents when they come to talk to
26   everyone today. To find out what happened to their son.
27   Our best friend! *(Silence while the other boys look at each*
28   *other guiltily.)*
29 MASON: It *is* going to be hard. What are we supposed to tell
30   them?
31 TANNER: Maybe we could say we didn't fire our guns either.
32 KEITH: I don't think they'll believe that Wes was out there
33   shooting all alone. That we all just ran around letting him
34   shoot at us.
35 MASON: Yeah. Me either.

1 TANNER: Maybe Wes shot his gun and it ricocheted off a rock
2   or something and hit him in the eye. Maybe it was his own
3   pellet that got him!
4 KEITH: It could've happened that way. We don't really know.
5 JACOB: I don't think they're going to be happy if we try to
6   blame Wes for what happened. Do you? *(Pause)*
7 KEITH: Well, who was closest to him when he started
8   screaming?
9 JACOB: I was. He was so close to where I was hiding. I thought
10   he'd found me! I kept waiting for him to shoot me, and then
11   he started screaming. I didn't know what was going on, but
12   I ran right over to him.
13 KEITH: Who came next? Both Tanner and Mason were there
14   when I got to you guys.
15 JACOB: I think it was Mason.
16 MASON: No! Tanner was already there when I got there. *(They*
17   *all turn to look at TANNER, like this has solved the issue.)*
18 TANNER: Wait a minute! That doesn't mean anything! Just
19   'cause I got there first — after Jacob — doesn't mean I
20   shot Wes!
21 MASON: Well, you would've been closest!
22 TANNER: Maybe I just run faster! You guys got there just
23   seconds after me! We were all right there! You are not
24   pinning this on me! *(Panicking)* And who believes Jacob
25   anyway? Doesn't it seem awfully fishy that he was the first
26   one to Wes but that he didn't fire his gun? Not one single
27   time? Doesn't that seem convenient? *(Now they all turn and*
28   *look at JACOB.)*
29 MASON: It *is* a little suspicious.
30 KEITH: Certainly makes for a great alibi!
31 JACOB: You're calling me a liar? First you call me a coward and
32   now I'm a liar?
33 TANNER: Well, it's not like you can prove your story, now is it?
34 KEITH: And you *were* the first one there.
35 JACOB: Guess what? I can prove it. *(Digs in pocket and then*

1   *slams down a handful of BBs onto the table.)* **Go on! Count**
2   **them! Exactly fifty pellets. The same number we all started**
3   **with.**

4   TANNER: That doesn't prove anything! You could've gotten
5   those at the store today. We could all go buy fifty pellets
6   and then say that we didn't fire our guns either. Then who
7   would Wes's parents believe?

8   JACOB: *(Standing up, angry)* You know what? You guys are
9   unbelievable! You can think and say what you want, but I
10   know the truth and that's all that matters. And you know
11   what? I'm not the one who's a coward now. It's you. All of
12   you. Afraid to tell the truth. *(Leaves. They all watch him.)*

13   KEITH: I don't know about you guys, but I think he was telling
14   the truth.

15   MASON: Me, too.

16   TANNER: He was pretty angry.

17   KEITH: Can you blame him? We got a little carried away.

18   MASON: I guess paranoia can do that to you.

19   TANNER: *(Looking at the group that's left)* So now it's down to three.

20   KEITH: I guess it really was one of us who shot Wes.

21   MASON: Yeah, but which one?

22   TANNER: Should we just draw straws? Let somebody take the
23   fall since we don't know who really did it?

24   MASON: What's that going to prove?

25   TANNER: I don't know. Maybe Wes's parents are out for blood.
26   Maybe they want one of us to get arrested or something.

27   MASON: I don't want to go to jail.

28   KEITH: It was an accident. Even Wes told them that. They're not
29   going to have us arrested.

30   MASON: You don't know that.

31   KEITH: I *do* know that. They're good people. They know we
32   wouldn't hurt Wes on purpose. They just want to hear what
33   really happened.

34   TANNER: Even if we don't have the answer? The one who really
35   did it?

1 KEITH: You know, I don't think it has to be *one* of us. We're just
2   going to have to take responsibility. All of us. Say how
3   sorry we are and live with the fact that it could've been any
4   one of us who did it.
5 MASON: Maybe ...
6 TANNER: You know, it could've been any one of us to lose an
7   eye, too.
8 KEITH: I know. It was pretty dumb to be shooting BBs at each
9   other like that. *(Pause.)*
10 TANNER: I wish I'd been afraid and hid like Jacob.
11 KEITH/MASON: Me, too.
12 TANNER: You know what? I bet Wes does, too. But that doesn't
13   change anything, does it? *(Stands up.)* Come on, we'd
14   better go talk to his parents.

Overbearing Mother

(2 Guys, 2 Girls)
CHARACTERS:

Danielle: Sierra's friend who tries to keep her calm about her grades and help her find a solution.

Sierra: Girl who gets a B and is freaking out because her mother expects only A's.

Alex: Acts like a goof-off but in the end thinks Sierra should just tell the truth.

Jordan: True goof-off who gets upset with Sierra's drama and believes the way out is to break the computer.

SETTING:

The two boys are talking in the hallway at school. Then the two girls come out of a classroom a few seconds later. Sierra is really upset.

1 DANIELLE: Seriously, I promise. It'll be OK. It's not that bad.

2 SIERRA: No it won't! My mom is going to kill me!

3 ALEX: What's going on?

4 JORDAN: *(To ALEX)* Get ready; here comes another of Sierra's
5   meltdowns over stupid things that don't matter. Just try to
6   act like you care.

7 DANIELLE: Sierra got a B in Algebra, and she's freaking out
8   about it. It's really not even a big deal.

9 SIERRA: No, I'm not, and even if I am, you would be too! My
10   mom is going to flip when she sees this. She thinks that
11   A's are the only way to go. If we ever get a B we're in *a lot*
12   of trouble.

13 JORDAN: Well, she wouldn't like my report card, then.

14 ALEX: Or mine. I, like, only get B's.

15 SIERRA: Can you guys get over it? I have a problem here, and
16   you're only worried about yourselves like always.

17 DANIELLE: OK, maybe you can just go talk to Mrs. Thompson
18   and see if you can get your grade raised.

19 SIERRA: We're talking about *Mrs. Thompson.* She doesn't
20   accept late work and there's no extra credit. Ever.

21 DANIELLE: Maybe she would this one time. You never know. It's
22   worth a try at least.

23 SIERRA: No way. It's so dumb, too. I always get hundreds in her
24   class! Then I was too busy practicing for my piano recital
25   and I forgot to study for that stupid quiz! One stupid F and
26   now I've got a B in her class! How can that even be
27   possible?

28 ALEX: She counts quizzes twice. It's so unfair.

29 SIERRA: She's probably just out to get me. Ever since teacher
30   appreciation. I mean it's an honest mistake. We have *so*
31   many teachers and it's easy to just forget one. I can tell
32   that ever since I forgot about her stupid present, she's
33   been acting different towards me. And of course the time I
34   blurt out that I forgot to study — pop quiz! Totally taking
35   advantage of the situation!

1 DANIELLE: Don't overreact. I always get A's and I didn't get her
2   a gift.
3 JORDAN: When I got a D on my report card, my mom freaked
4   and made me go to tutoring. It stunk. The tutors think they
5   know everything. I hated it.
6 DANIELLE: You're not helping.
7 ALEX: This is so stupid; it's a B. My mom is happy when I get
8   B's.
9 SIERRA: Well, your mom wasn't valedictorian in college, was
10   she? And she doesn't expect you to be *exactly* like her,
11   does she?
12 ALEX: *(Sarcastically)* OK. Sorry.
13 JORDAN: I don't understand why it's a big deal. It's only
14   midterms; it doesn't even count.
15 SIERRA: In my mom's head it does. She frames every single
16   report card that we get back. Doesn't matter whether it's
17   a midterm or not. To her, they all count. She switches
18   them out every grading period.
19 DANIELLE: It's true. I've seen them. It's like the wall of fame.
20 SIERRA: Or in my case, the wall of *shame!*
21 ALEX: You're so dramatic, Sierra.
22 SIERRA: Dramatic? My sisters all are going to have their
23   midterms put in a frame and hung on the wall, and mine
24   will be thrown away. I'll probably be grounded for life and
25   my mother will look at me with pure disappointment;
26   wondering where she went wrong in raising me. She will tell
27   all her friends, "Oh, look how smart Lisa and Gretchen
28   are!" and then she'll look at me and just shake her head.
29 DANIELLE: I've seen that look before, too! Your mom does that
30   whole I'm-so-disappointed-in-you look absolutely perfect!
31 SIERRA: All because Mrs. Thompson won't give me a chance!
32   All she had to do was round my grade up one point! One
33   stinking little point and I'd have an A on my midterm. I
34   think she's just out to get me and make me fail.
35 JORDAN: A B is not failing. Anyway, Mrs. Thompson is the only

1   nice teacher in this hallway. How can you not like her?

2   SIERRA: Have you not been listening? Gosh, Jordan! You're so

3   stupid.

4   JORDAN: Really? Because I'm not the one with a B in Mrs.

5   Thompson's class. Mrs. Thompson actually likes me and

6   always gives me A's.

7   DANIELLE: *(Ignoring JORDAN)* Sierra, it's not that big of a deal.

8   So your midterm doesn't get put in a frame and hung on

9   the wall. And so you might get grounded for a little while

10   — it's just one time.

11 SIERRA: How can you say that? I *have* to have my midterm on

12   the wall. My sisters can't be the only people getting praised

13   for their good grades. They'll be impossible to live with, as

14   if they aren't already! They'll be so happy that I messed up.

15   I always have higher grades, am better at sports, and play

16   the piano way better than them! If I slip up just one time,

17   I'll never hear the end of it!

18 ALEX: Well, it's not like they're perfect.

19 SIERRA: They'll seem that way now, won't they? The perfect

20   daughters. I'll be the black sheep of the family. The family

21   dunce. They probably won't even let me eat at the table

22   with them.

23 JORDAN: Oh, please. One B is not going to get you disowned

24   from your family.

25 ALEX: Really. One B is not going to kill you.

26 SIERRA: You don't know that. I could die of my mom's

27   disappointment.

28 DANIELLE: Maybe it's time for your sisters to have a moment to

29   shine. Believe me, I live in my sister's shadow, and that's

30   not a great place to be. I'd give anything for her to mess up.

31 SIERRA: Well, this isn't about you, Danielle, now is it? You're

32   always try to make everything be about you. So can we get

33   back to how I'm going to get this grade up? *(DANIELLE*

34   *looks angry.)*

35 JORDAN: What if you don't show her and say you haven't

1   gotten your midterm yet and you get it up to an A before
2   she notices.

3 SIERRA: Are you an idiot? My mom checks my grades every
4   night online. That wouldn't work.

5 ALEX: What if you tell her they made a mistake and you really
6   do have all A's?

7 SIERRA: Uh, I don't know. I'm not a very good liar.

8 JORDAN: Really? 'Cause you're a great actor.

9 ALEX: You — not a good liar? You told me you had a second
10   house in Hawaii the first time we met.

11 SIERRA: We were in third grade! Everybody lies in third grade!
12   And besides, my parents *were* thinking about buying land
13   in Hawaii.

14 JORDAN: Yeah, just like they were *thinking* about becoming
15   missionaries in Africa that one year.

16 SIERRA: Well, they were. Can I help it if they change their minds
17   a lot?

18 ALEX: And the time you told me that Tom Cruise was your
19   uncle. I met your uncle, and he doesn't look a thing like
20   Tom Cruise.

21 SIERRA: OK. This isn't helping. Let's stay focused, OK? So how
22   is my mom not going to know about the B when she
23   checks my grades every night?

24 JORDAN: Ooooh! Break your computer! Then blame it on one
25   of your perfect sisters.

26 DANIELLE: *(Perks up at this idea. She'd love to do that to her sister.)*
27   Good idea! Then your sisters can get in trouble and *they*
28   can get that disappointed look! *(ALEX and JORDAN high five*
29   *each other.)*

30 SIERRA: I am not going to break my computer! You guys are so
31   stupid!

32 JORDAN: Not as stupid as your face.

33 ALEX: Ooooh, burn. *(ALEX and JORDAN high five each other again.)*

34 SIERRA: You guys are so immature. I can't even believe I'm
35   friends with you!

1 DANIELLE: I know! Why don't you say that you should go out
2   for dinner? That way when you get home, you can stay on
3   the computer all night and your mom won't be able to get
4   on to check your grades.
5 SIERRA: I guess that could work. I'll tell her I'm working on
6   research for a project. And I'll take forever to eat at the
7   restaurant. Maybe I could even hang out in the bathroom
8   for awhile and pretend that my stomach hurts!
9 ALEX: That sounds like a lot of work. Why don't you just tell
10   your mom? She might not like it, but she'll be happy that
11   you didn't lie about it. You can't hide your grades forever,
12   so you're going to have to tell her eventually. Why not come
13   clean now?
14 SIERRA: Eventually is better than now.
15 ALEX: I just think that that would be the right thing to do.
16 SIERRA: Since when did you become Mr. Goody-two-shoes?
17 ALEX: Say what you want, but lying or hiding it is only going to
18   make it worse. Trust me.
19 SIERRA: This from the guy that wanted me to break my
20   computer and blame it on my sisters.
21 ALEX: You know I was just kidding about that. Well, I have to
22   get to class. See you guys later. Sierra, I think you should
23   tell your mom the truth. Even if you get away with it, you
24   know lying about it is going to eat you up. *(Leaves.)*
25 SIERRA: What got into him? He's so stupid. Acting like Dr. Phil
26   or something.
27 DANIELLE: I think I'm with him. You should just tell your mom.
28   I mean, I know you'll get grounded and everything, but I
29   think it'd be better to just face it.
30 SIERRA: What?! You just told me to stall at dinner and then
31   your boyfriend thinks I should tell the truth and all of a
32   sudden you do, too? How convenient! And are you
33   forgetting? My midterm won't get hung on the wall and my
34   parents will be disappointed.
35 DANIELLE: OK. First, he's not my boyfriend. But I think he has

1   a point. And second, this whole thing is ridiculous. It's one

2   grade. Tell the truth and then get over it. Your mom is not

3   as bad as you make her sound. *(Leaves.)*

4 SIERRA: *(To JORDAN)* Are you with them too?

5 JORDAN: I still think you should break the computer. It could

6   work in so many ways!

7 SIERRA: Oh, just get out of here!

About the Author

This is Rebecca Young's fourth book for teens. Regarding her inspiration for the numerous plays and monologues she's written so far, she says, "I have three girls; two of which are still teenagers, one just barely out of that age range. It's all about comedy and tragedy around my house. Believe me, there's not much else in between." Friends and family (she won't dare say who), television, and just a plain old overactive imagination help Rebecca create a wide array of drama-filled topics from which to choose.

When she's not writing books, Rebecca writes and directs drama for middle and high school students at her church. She co-founded a group called One Voice who travels annually to perform at various churches. It is a great passion of hers to combine writing and working with youth.

Rebecca currently works in a totally "non-dramatic" profession as a technical trainer in Lexington, Kentucky. She has a B.A. in Communications/Marketing from the University of Kentucky.

Ms. Young lives with her husband (Frank), three wonderful and dramatic daughters (Heather, Kristina, and Ashley), and two cats. (The cats have names but are more often than not called Orange Kitty and Gray Kitty. And lately, "Bad Kitty" because one has been having issues!)

Whether you are an actor or a writer, she suggests this quote as a daily mantra: "You aren't finished when you lose; you are finished when you quit."

Order Form

Meriwether Publishing Ltd.
PO Box 7710
Colorado Springs, CO 80933-7710
Phone: 800-937-5297 Fax: 719-594-9916
Website: www.meriwether.com

Please send me the following books:

_____ **Ten-Minute Plays for**   **$17.95**
Middle School Performers #BK-B305
by Rebecca Young
Plays for a variety of cast sizes

_____ **101 Monologues for Middle School Actors**   **$15.95**
#BK-B303
by Rebecca Young
Including duologues and triologues

_____ **Famous Fantasy Character Monologs**   **$15.95**
#BK-B286
by Rebecca Young
Starring the Not-So-Wicked Witch and more

_____ **100 Great Monologs #BK-B276**   **$15.95**
by Rebecca Young
A collection of monologs, duologs and triologs for actors

_____ **Winning Monologs for Young Actors**   **$15.95**
#BK-B127
by Peg Kehret
Honest-to-life monologs for young actors

_____ **Sixty Comedy Duet Scenes for Teens**   **$16.95**
#BK-B302
by Laurie Allen
Real-life situations for laughter

_____ **Thirty Short Comedy Plays for Teens**   **$16.95**
#BK-B292
by Laurie Allen
Plays for a variety of cast sizes

These and other fine Meriwether Publishing books are available at
your local bookstore or direct from the publisher. Prices subject to
change without notice. Check our website or call for current prices.

Name: _____ e-mail: _____

Organization name: _____

Address: _____

City: _____ State: _____

Zip: _____ Phone: _____

    ❏ **Check enclosed**

    ❏ **Visa / MasterCard / Discover / Am. Express #** _____

*   Expiration*
Signature: _____ *date:* _____ / _____
       (required for credit card orders)

Colorado residents: Please add 3% sales tax.
Shipping: Include $3.95 for the first book and 75¢ for each additional book ordered.

    ❏ *Please send me a copy of your complete catalog of books and plays.*